CW01650393

sur purchase:

Patience

CHOICES

by

PATIENCE ADDISON

Unless otherwise indicated all scripture quotations are taken from the updated Living Bible. Scripture quotations marked (TLB) are taken from The Living Bible. Scripture quotations marked (NIV) are taken from the New International Version and those marked (KJV) are taken from the King James Version of the Holy Bible. Scripture quotations marked (ICB) are taken from the International Children's Bible. Scripture quotations marked (NKJV) are taken from the New King James Version.

The Oxford online dictionary and Collins Harper online dictionary have been used as reference sources.

CHOICES

ISBN: 978-1-7391721-0-7

Published by HOMI Publishing.

Printed in the UK by Imprintdigital.com

Seychelles Farm, Upton Pyne, EX5 5HY, UK.

DEDICATION

This book is dedicated to all those who seek to make the right choices in life, choices that will enable them to make the most out of life rather than leave them in constant regret and with painful consequences.

Table of Contents

Chapter 1. Believing In The Existence Of God 1

Chapter 2 Maintaining Innocence 6

Chapter 3 Life Or Death 12

Chapter 4 Offering.. 17

Chapter 5 Friendship 22

Chapter 6 Standout 28

Chapter 7 Obedience To God 34

Chapter 8 Reap What You Sow 41

Chapter 9 Respecting Boundaries...................................... 46

Chapter 10 Blessings And Curses...................................... 51

Chapter 11 Unity 55

Chapter 12 Separation.. 60

Chapter 13 Choice By Flesh Or Faith................................. 64

Chapter 14 Helping Others.. 68

Chapter 15 To Be Hopeful 73

Chapter 16 Self Help Or God's Help 77

Chapter 17 Circumcision/ Cutting Off Old Life 82

Chapter 18 Showing Hospitality 88

Chapter 19 To Look Back Or Not 94

Chapter 20 Maintaining Integrity 98

Chapter 21 Patience/ Impatience.................................. 102

Chapter 22 Passing God's Test 106

Chapter 23 Giving A Befitting Burial 112

Chapter 24 Choosing The Right Partner 117

Chapter 25 Present Satisfaction 124

Chapter 26 Prospering In The Midst Of Adversities 130

Chapter 27 Hard Work 136

Chapter 28 Obedience To Parents 141

Chapter 29 Deception 148

Chapter 30 Envy Or Jealousy 155

Chapter 31 Tolerance 159

Chapter 32 Reconciliation 164

Chapter 33 Running At Your Own Pace 172

Chapter 34 Self-Control 177

Chapter 35 Showing Gratitude To God 181

Chapter 36 Moving On In Life 188

Chapter 37 Hatred 193

Chapter 38 Judging Others 199

Chapter 39 Faithful Service 205

Chapter 40 Putting Your Gift To Use 211

Chapter 41 Saving Mentality 217

Chapter 42 Learning From Past Mistakes 223

Chapter 43 Honesty 229

Chapter 44 Leadership 234

Chapter 45 Forgiveness 241

Chapter 46 Relocation 247

Chapter 47 Saviour 252

Chapter 48 A Blissful Farewell 258

Chapter 49 Parent's Blessings 263

Chapter 50 Fulfilling A Promise 268

ACKNOWLEDGEMENTS

I am eternally grateful to the almighty God for his mercy and grace, and for counting me worthy to serve in his vineyard.

I would also like to express my sincere gratitude to my editor Patricia J. Markall BA (Hons), MSc. for taking time out of her busy schedule, and during these challenging times, to edit this book.

My thanks, also go to my husband, Rev. Richard Donkor, for his enormous input, our son Ithel, my mother Flora Padi, and my family and friends for all their support and encouragement in writing this book and in all my endeavours.

Finally, to the body of Christ, I appreciate your prayers, advice and support throughout my walk with Christ.

God bless you all.

INTRODUCTION

Choices in life are inevitable. God has given each one of us the will to choose. We are all, therefore, the result of the choices we make. We choose at crucial points of our lives to feel, speak and act in the way we do. The company we keep, the friends, jobs and ambitions we have are due to the choices we make and goals we set ourselves. We can, however, make right or wrong choices. But whatever choices we make, we are responsible for them and the consequences that come with them.

We get to find out on a daily basis that, some choices we make bring great benefits to us, whereas others limit us in so many ways. Others give us pleasure for a short period of time while some may give us lasting satisfaction. Still, all the choices we make in turn lead us into making other similar choices and unless we pause to take stock of life, we can be particularly destroyed by these choices. We however find out from the word of God, those choices made in accordance with the will of God give us more fulfilment in life. Whereas those not, give us pleasure but for a time and leave us unfulfilled.

The choices we make reveal and further form our character. They tell others a lot about who we truly are and are a true reflection of the kind of life we live. Should we live unfulfilled lives in which we keep starting off and getting off at the same place where we started in a repeated cycle, then the choices we are making need to be reconsidered. On the other hand, if the lives we live have a beginning and are moving towards a purposeful direction in a linear pattern, we are probably making the right choices. Much the same, our choices form our character and make us into the people we are.

It is important, therefore, that choices are made in the right way, according to God's will, as he created life and has the instructions for its use. Abiding by God's instructions, enables us to make the right choices, thereby enjoying a fulfilled and prosperous life.

This book consists of 50 carefully and prayerfully selected choices, each one of us is bound to make in life. Each choice is based on a theme in a chapter of the book of Genesis. Genesis is the principal book of the Christian bible that presents to us the beginning of all things; life and death, marriage and family life, success and failure, just to mention a few. Unsurprisingly, it is the first of the 66 books of the Christian bible. It introduces diverse choices one can make, hence its use as the primary source of information for this book. It may be beneficial for the reader to study each chapter of the book of Genesis before reading each chapter of this book.

This book gives the reader the opportunity to study all 50 chapters of the book of Genesis. It also reminds them of some of the choices made by the people in the bible and the consequences that befell them. They are choices we make in our lifetime and the fact that God has allowed them in his word means they are important to him, and he wants us to learn from them so we can make the right choices and make the most out of our lives.

CHAPTER 1

BELIEVING IN THE EXISTENCE OF GOD

In the beginning God created the heavens and the earth. (NIV)

Genesis 1:1

MESSAGE AND LEARNING

"In the beginning God…". We are straight away presented with God in the first sentence in the book of Genesis. This chapter introduces God to us. It primarily centres on God as the creator of all things. In other words, it reveals the existence of God through creation to us. It talks about the fact that; God begun all things and reminds us that God is eternal. He has always been there and will always be there. God existed before creation and still exists to this day. Whoever wants to find God, must first believe that he exists and that he rewards those who earnestly seek him. It is through our earnest seeking of God that we find him. That is, if we begin by believing that he is there, getting to know him and walk in his ways, then we can experience his existence.

Some people do not believe in the existence of God, for instance, atheists. In as much as they do not believe that God exists, Genesis 1, talks about how the earth was originally formless, dark and empty and God's ability to create and make all things good and beautiful. This makes it clear, that God is not a thing, a force or an idea. Thus, we get to learn of God as a person. He has a mind to think, a will to decide and a heart to feel. God therefore decided to create the earth, planned how he wanted it to be and what he would be happy to see. Then, he went ahead to create it the way he wanted it. In addition to that, we find out in this chapter how good, loving, powerful, creative, and orderly God is and the fact that he speaks through creation.

To help us in our understanding of the existence of God, let us start by thinking about the phones we use. What comes to mind when we think about their existence? Do we believe they were made by someone and that they just did not show up on the shelves in the shops for us to go and pick them up or otherwise? I believe most of us will agree that someone or a group of people sat down, thought about the need for them and went ahead to make them. In the same way as we believe our phones have a maker, the whole world was made by a creator who the bible tells us in Genesis chapter 1 is God. This chapter of the bible presents God to us as the creator of the heavens and the earth with all that is within it, thereby telling us of his existence. Further chapters also prove the existence of God through the experiences people had with him. Besides these two ways, the word of God, reveals his existence to us. Thus, God's existence has been made known to man through his word as we read it, through creation and experiences we or others have had, which proves he exists.

The belief we have in the existence of God and that he created all things gives us the assurance that he owns everything including us. Likewise, it teaches us that if God created us, then he alone has the instructions for our lives, which he has given to us in his word just as a maker of a phone has instructions for its use. Should we want to make the most of life therefore, it will be wise to live according to the maker's instructions.

Having been introduced in this very first chapter of the book of Genesis about God's existence, we have a choice to make as to whether to believe in his existence or not. Our choice of believing in his existence helps us in our search for him, which leads to us finding him. This choice gives us all the rewards and fulfilment we seek in life. On the other hand, by not believing in his existence, we are not encouraged in any way to seek and find him.

Consequently, we miss out on all the rewards he has planned for us. Do you believe that God exists or not?

CHAPTER QUESTIONS

&

THEMES FOR THOUGHT

- Is there anything around you (that is in God's creation) that makes you think God exists.
- How would you explain to someone who doubts the existence of God that God truly exists?
- Having learnt that God speaks, creates, he is orderly, powerful and good, can you identify a verse from this chapter which shows any of the listed attributes/attitudes of God and explain your understanding relating it to the chosen attributes/attitudes.

YOU CAN SUMMARISE YOUR THOUGHTS

YOU CAN REVISIT YOUR THOUGHTS

CHAPTER 2

MAINTAINING INNOCENCE

But the Lord God gave him this warning: "You may freely eat any fruit in the garden, except fruit from the tree of the knowledge of good and evil. If you eat of its fruit, you will surely die.

Genesis 2: 16-17

MESSAGE AND LEARNING

God is all-knowing. Nothing in all creation is hidden from his sight. Everything is uncovered and laid bare before his eyes. He knows the past, the present and even the future. What's more, he is a good God.

God's goodness is shown throughout creation. His goodness can be seen in his willingness and choice to create man in his own image, nothing less than who he is: that is his likeness. Think about this, God wanted man to be like him: think like him, speak like him and do things the way he does them. So, he created a garden in the East called Eden and there, he placed man to care for it. God gave man the dominion over all that he had created and the authority to name all the animals so man could be like him and share in his authority.

With God being all knowing, he knew straight away that it was not good for man to live alone. He knew the need man had and made a companion suitable for him. He gave everything that is good, freely to man without withholding anything man needed from him, including the tree of life and man's will so he could freely make the choice he wanted for himself. To be candid, if God showed man this extent of love and goodness, then it was right if man did the same in return to God through obedience. But, as stated earlier in this paragraph, God wanted man to do things out of his own free will without being forced to do it, for he is a good God. The only thing that God forbade was man eating off the tree of knowledge of good and evil. For although one could gain knowledge of good by eating from it, knowledge gained was not only good but also of evil.

The word knowledge simply means personal experience of something or someone. Eating from the tree of knowledge of good and evil meant experiencing what is good but also what is evil, which God in his love did not want man to have experience of. As once a person has experienced evil, he or she can no longer retain innocence of it. If we do a wrong thing, we can never be the same as we were before. We gain knowledge of that wrong we did and are no longer innocent of it. If a person steals, they know what it is like to steal. They may be forgiven but would have lost their innocence. Trying things out for ourselves in a way of finding out what is good or bad, makes us experience evil at a stage in our lives. Thus, could make us lose our innocence of those bad experiences and when this happens, we are never the same again. As already mentioned, God in his love did not want man to experience evil. He wanted man to retain his innocence of evil. He wanted man to trust him to decide what was right or wrong for him. He put the tree in man's reach communicating that he retains moral authority over man. Also conveying the message that we do not decide for ourselves what is right or wrong but need to trust him to tell us what is right or wrong.

Let us think about it in this way. When we were babies, our parents in their love were so protective of us, they did not want us to eat food that had gone off, so we continue to keep our good health and not become ill. They saw it as their duty to give us all the good things they had, whilst preventing us from the bad things that could harm us. By leaving us to eat anything we wanted and try out food that is good or bad for ourselves, would have meant us experiencing at some point in our lives an upset stomach due to eating bad food. We would have gained knowledge of how it felt, experiencing this, which is not what they would like for us to experience. This would in turn mean we would have lost our innocence of such a bad experience. In a way, it was our parents' way of helping us maintain good health and not have knowledge of what it feels like to experience this. This example can be likened to God's way of helping us maintain our innocence in evil. God wanted man to be innocent of the knowledge of evil so that he could enjoy his creation by trusting him to tell him what is right or wrong. However, man disobeyed God and lost his innocence of evil by eating from the tree of the knowledge of good and evil. This brought shame, punishment, separation from God and ultimately death.

Every time we lose our innocence, we experience shame, feel lonely and guilty of the things we did and in most cases are punished for the acts we committed. But then, by maintaining our innocence, we live with a guilt free conscience and are happier. God still wants us to maintain our innocence of all the bad things around us which the bible calls sin. So, this way we can avoid their effects on our lives. Examples of which are stealing, telling lies, disobedience and being envious of others. He wants us to trust him when he tells us these things can destroy us, without us having to experience them ourselves and losing our innocence of them. Not to mention the shame, punishment and other bad consequences that come with them.

Will you make a choice of maintaining your innocence of the bad things you have not yet experienced but have been told are not good? For example, if you have been told by your parents not to steal – that is a bad act that they would not want you to experience. In this way, helping you to maintain your innocence of it. Now then, will you make this choice and be innocent of evil or not?

CHAPTER QUESTIONS

&

THEMES FOR THOUGHT

- What does it mean to maintain innocence?
- Do you think it is still necessary to maintain innocence of bad experiences?
- Can you state two things you would like to maintain innocence of?
- To help you in answering this question, think of things your parents, grandparents or teachers have told you not to do because they have bad consequences and you have not yet done. Also, what are some of the things the word of God tells you are wrong?

YOU CAN SUMMARISE YOUR THOUGHTS

YOU CAN REVISIT YOUR THOUGHTS

CHAPTER 3

LIFE OR DEATH

"Of course, we may eat it," the woman told him. "It's only the fruit from the tree at the centre of the garden that we are not to eat. God says we mustn't eat it or even touch it, or we will die." (TLB)

Genesis 3: 2-3

MESSAGE AND LEARNING

God is holy. He hates sin as sin spoils all the good he has created. For this reason, he judges sin. One who is found guilty of sin is liable to punishment, the ultimate of which is death. God, however, wishes above all things, that we will all live and have eternal life. Therefore, he sent his only begotten son to die in our place, so that we may live forever. For us to receive the life God offers, means parting company with sin and a willingness to stay free from it forever.

But the trouble is, Satan is always finding ways and means to cause us to sin against God. He particularly does this by causing us to doubt what God has said with our minds, desire to do the very things God dislikes with our hearts and causes us to do what will hurt God with our will, that is to sin. Every day presents us each, with the choice of life or death. The choices we make determines whether we have life or death now and in eternity. The choices we make concerning situations that befall us each time are as a result of who we are (that is whether we are enslaved by sin or not) and whether we love life or death. For whoever lives under the influence of sin makes choices that lead to death and whoever loves life makes choices to preserve it rather than lose it.

From the second chapter of Genesis, we learnt that God gave Adam and Eve a warning not to eat off the tree of the knowledge of good and evil. For once they ate off it; they experienced evil and hence had to die. They were presented with a choice of either eating everything in the garden including the tree of life, so they could go on living but not the tree of knowledge of good and evil which led to death. Sadly enough, they chose to eat off the tree of knowledge of good and evil. They disobeyed God, they were rebellious to his instructions and opposed his authority by eating from the tree of knowledge of good and evil, hence had to die.

The bible presents death to us in two ways. One of which is spiritual death which occurs instantly when one commits evil or sins against God. This death is also known as separation from God. For God hates sin and a choice to live with sin means a choice to live away from him. Since God is the source of life, by exhausting the life already received without replenishing it, led to death once one got separated from him.

We realise that spiritual death however sets in motion the physical death. Here is the situation in which, Adam and Eve had disobeyed God by eating off the tree of knowledge of good and evil and were separated from God. Not only that, but they were also banished from God's beautiful garden and lost access to the tree of life which could have made them go on living. They lost access to the only one tree which was meant to keep their mortal bodies alive. Hence, had to physically die.

God has however, promised to give each of us life when we realise and admit our sins, thus, turning back to him for forgiveness. This way we receive the life he gives us now and in eternity. We get to be with him here on earth and also eat off the tree of life and live forever with him till eternity.

No matter where we are in life, we can choose to receive life again instead of death by turning back to God and willingly receive from him the life he offers. God has however given us individually the will to choose between life and death. We can choose life and live with God in eternity or death and be separated from him in this life and the next forever. Which choice do you make? Life or death?

CHAPTER QUESTIONS

&

THEMES FOR THOUGHT

- Why is it important to choose life over death?
- By what means were Adam and Eve able to choose death over life?
- How can we avoid the same mistakes Adam and Eve committed and the subsequent consequences?

YOU CAN SUMMARISE YOUR THOUGHTS

YOU CAN REVISIT YOUR THOUGHTS

CHAPTER 4

OFFERING

"Later, Cain brought a gift to God. He brought some food from the ground. Abel brought the best parts of his best sheep. The Lord accepted Abel and his gift. But God did not accept Cain and his gift. Cain became very angry and looked unhappy." (ICB)

Genesis 4: 3-5

MESSAGE AND LEARNING

It is an act of worship to offer unto God. In offering to God, we fulfil our duty to him. Doing so pleases him and ensures we receive continual supplies of his goodness. God is and has always been the first giver of all things good. Freely he gives us life, the air we breathe, the sun that lightens our day, our gifts and talents and the power to gain wealth. It is only when we come to the realisation that God owns all things and that he has freely given us all we have. We appreciate his gifts and also the need to offer unto him. We can offer to God our love, time, substance and effort. Literally, everything God has given to us can be offered back to him by us. We can also offer directly to God or indirectly to him, when we do things for our neighbours or community. This gives us the understanding that by showing kindness to the people around us and caring for our community, we preserve his creation, and this makes him happy. Also, our offering teaches us and others not to be selfish as freely we have received, and freely shall we give.

Anytime we offer something to someone, it is up to the person to either accept or reject what has been offered to them. One reason for this is that, although some of the things we offer might be of use to the people we offer it to, most often than not they might not need them. We often find out most offerings, stem from practices, customs or acts that have been performed in accordance with tradition. Hence, many offer not because they want to but because they must. Think of the many times you have offered a gift to someone at Christmas without finding out what their need is and have found out later in the year that the very gift you offered has stayed in a corner unused, or has been recycled to another person or has found its way to the charity shop? Do you think these acts of offerings were needed? Besides from what has been offered may not be what is needed, but it may also not be very pleasant. Especially in instances when the person being given the gift, finds out very little effort was put into what they had received, the person who bought the gift could have put more thought and effort into the gift process.

We are told in this chapter that both Cain and Abel offered unto God. God did not ask them to give to him, neither were they forced into giving unto God. However, while Cain brought some food from the ground to God, Abel offered the best parts of his best flock. From their actions after God's reception to their gifts, we learn they each expected God to accept their gifts. However, God accepted Abel's gift, but declined Cain's. Abel offered unto God in the right way, but Cain did not.

From this, we first learn that whenever we offer unto God, he not only accepts or rejects this but also the one who offers it. This means that the way in which we present our gifts to God is equally as important as what we offer. The intentions for which we give and our attitudes to giving contributes to whether our gifts will be accepted by God. This is because our thoughts concerning our giving affect the way in which we give and what we give. Whenever we give to someone, we put thought into it; in that, we think about whom they are, our relationship with them, how much they mean to us and what they will or will not like. It is by doing this that; we give, knowing our gifts will be accepted.

Should we be really willing to offer, we will do so without holding back but rather offer our best possible gift with an aim of it being accepted. Knowing this, will open many more doors of opportunity for us.

Abel offered the best of his best to God and his offering was accepted. Out of the abundance God has given us, we can in turn offer to him. But the decision is ours to either give him some of what we have or the best of the best of it. For example, a batch of fallen apples from a tree, half of them are fine and half of them are bruised. Your offering would be the good unbruised apples, in other words giving the best of the best. Thus, best offerings reflect people who are giving gifts with a lot of love and thought and of their own free will.

Will you be willing to offer the best of your best to God?

CHAPTER QUESTIONS

&

THEMES FOR THOUGHT

- What are some of the things we could offer unto God?
- What can you do to make your offering acceptable unto God?
- What 2 things do you choose to offer unto God from today?
- Why have you chosen to offer them?

YOU CAN SUMMARISE YOUR THOUGHTS

YOU CAN REVISIT YOUR THOUGHTS

CHAPTER 5

FRIENDSHIP

"Enoch walked faithfully with God; then he was no more, because God took him away." (NIV)

Genesis 5:24

MESSAGE AND LEARNING

Man is a relational being. We were not created to live in isolation but to relate with the creator and his creation. It is in our relationships that we find the meaning of life. Our relationships differ to an extent depending on whom and how we know the other person. Examples of relations one can have are family, friends and colleagues and all these have other sub relationships. For instance, parent and child relationships and husband and wife relationships fall under family relationships. This chapter however focuses on friendship.

Friendship is a mutual affection between two or more people. It is essentially a thing of minds that like each other. We like our friends because in a way, they are just like us. They think and behave in ways like us. Because of this, our friends share our views, and this makes us have similar tastes and outlooks. Thus, is a way of forming a mutual bond in which we share the same aspects and prospects in life. As already highlighted previously in this book, we are responsible for the friendship and company we keep. However, our choice of friends is probably one of the biggest choices we make in life that affects our character now and determines our future life.

In Genesis 5, we learn about Enoch's close relationship with God throughout his lifetime. They must have shared things in common which made them spend most of their time together. Enoch must have ensured that he did the very things that made God happy and likewise enjoyed all God had given in return throughout their friendship in order to keep the relationship alive. just as we, enjoy good times with our friends without wanting it to end; God had to take Enoch away with him. God must have enjoyed the relationship he had with Enoch to take him from this world to be with him, so Enoch could dwell with him forever in a better place.

The passage presents to us, three main learning opportunities. Firstly, our friends can impact our lives either positively or negatively. Secondly, they can influence our choices in life. Thirdly, they can determine where we end up in the future.

Our friends can have a great influence on our thoughts and actions to a great extent. In that, through spending time with them, they can rub off some of their good and bad habits on us and vice versa. For example, if you have a friend who is always fond of telling lies, you will sooner or later find out you have learnt and are practicing this bad habit. Much the same, if your friend is an honest person, you naturally walk in honesty. But this also depends on which of you has the greater influence on the other. If you are privileged therefore, to have a friend who has a good character, then, you will be at a gain should he or she have a greater influence on you. The bible therefore advises us to be wise in choosing our friends as by keeping bad company, we can ruin our good morals. While on the other hand, we gain wisdom by keeping company with the wise.

The impact our friends have on our thoughts and actions further influence the choices we make each day. Essentially, we like our friends because we get on well with them, for they do the things we like: the things we love to do, those that make us happy. When our friends do the things we enjoy, we in turn do what will make them happy hence keeping the relationship alive. When our friends are happy, we are too and vice versa. The things we do for our friends can however be either right or wrong so long as we please them in doing so. Hence, the reasons why we should choose our friends wisely, as by doing things to please them, we could end up doing the wrong things rather than the right things which can ruin our lives and leave us with regrets.

We also realise that when our friends do things that make us happy, we enjoy their company and spend most of our time with them without wanting to depart from each other. This is how most people follow their friends, spending a lot of time with them and their ending is either a happy or sad one depending on how and where they have been led.

In choosing our friends therefore, it will be wise if we consider certain qualities of a good friend. Does the person love you as you are no matter what is going on and, would they be willing to help bring out the best in you, rather than cause your worst qualities to be more prominent? Is the person someone you will be comfortable around, one who will accept your worst and give you earnest counsel to become your best? Do they have your best interests at heart, with the readiness to support you in times when you need help the most? Do they celebrate the success of others rather than act in an envious or jealous manner when others succeed? Should you answer yes to most of or all these questions, you probably are choosing or have a good friend. Through my study of the Christian bible, I have learnt that good friends are the ones who will always be your friend and stand with you through thick and thin. They are the ones who will always be frank with you and tell you the truth. They give you advice that is best for you and will benefit you and always treat you right and tell you when you are wrong.

Well then, are you in the process of choosing a friend? Do you know them well enough? Have you considered the impact they can have on the decisions and choices you make? Do you realise your ultimate destination in the future could be determined by the friends you keep? What choice do you make, from this point on when it comes to choosing your friends?

CHAPTER QUESTIONS

&

THEMES FOR THOUGHT

- What makes it so easy for our friends to influence us?
- Give examples of some characteristics that will help you identify a good friend?
- What are the benefits of being friends with God?

YOU CAN SUMMARISE YOUR THOUGHTS

YOU CAN REVISIT YOUR THOUGHTS

CHAPTER 6

STANDOUT

"The Lord observed the extent of human wickedness on the earth, and he saw that everything they thought or imagined was consistently and totally evil. So, the Lord was sorry he had ever made them and put them on the earth. It broke his heart. And the Lord said, "I will wipe this human race I have created from the face of the earth. Yes, and I will destroy every living thing—all the people, the large animals, the small animals that scurry along the ground, and even the birds of the sky. I am sorry I ever made them." But Noah found favour with the Lord. This is the account of Noah and his family. Noah was a righteous man, the only blameless person living on earth at the time, and he walked in close fellowship with God." (NLT)

Genesis 6: 5-9

MESSAGE AND LEARNING

We live in a world today where we are faced with difficult times. Hence, there is so much wickedness, aggression and greed to overindulge oneself with the riches of this world. To this extent, many are consistently and totally evil. Furthermore, the love for money and ourselves, being cruel and having no interest in what is good as long as we get what we want, is normal to us in our daily lives. These create enormous pressures around us and make us want to conform to what everyone else does rather than being independent and standing out from the crowd. At times, we may feel we will be despised should we stand out from the rest of the people doing the wrong things. Other times, for fear that we will be hated for exhibiting a better way while exposing bad ways makes us choose not to be different. So, we go with the flow and follow the crowd, doing the wrong things.

My understanding of a person who stands out like this is therefore one who has a high moral standard of living. One who aims to be good and not just say or do good things when they feel like it. Such a person promotes the good things around them and makes them grow while preventing the bad things they do not want to see grow. Their greatest ambition is to live right than to acquire power or wealth. They are merciful in their dealings and always seek to give others the chance to do well.

It is however simply, not nice being the odd one out in a group. The pressures of what other people may say or think are so much that it draws us into wanting to be like everyone else. Many therefore compromise their beliefs of what is morally right, thereby adjusting their behaviour and lowering their moral standards, to meet that of the world we live in. If people around us are using wrong means to amass wealth and get to top positions, then, it is okay for us to do likewise. If everyone agrees, what has been done to me is unpardonable, then, I see no wrong in not forgiving whoever wronged me. If people easily get away with the evil they do, then I can be reckless in my dealings and also get away with it too.

Standing out from other people makes us terribly unpopular. More so, when we stand up for what we believe to be right and true, we are taunted, and it causes us much hurt. Hence, we at times choose to go with the flow rather than choose to stand out from the crowd.

Sometimes when we go along with the wrong things around us, we gradually loose our good morals and our reputation. When we lose our good morals and reputation, it is difficult and almost impossible to get it back again. We then lack the knowledge of the fact that, even though people may not like us and may despise us for being different in what we stand up for, what we believe is right, we are respected if we are different in that sense. Likewise, we can affect other people around us to behave in a better way should we be different.

We learn from this chapter that people in Noah's generation did things that made God destroy the world they lived in. They may have forgotten they were tenants and not landlords hence, they always did things in a way to upset God, who owns the earth and its fullness. They played no part in building it but did things that brought the world they lived in, to an end. Hence, destroying it. Noah however, stood out from the rest of the people in his time when the thoughts and deeds of the people in his time were constantly and continually evil. He believed and stood for what was right without compromising his beliefs for any of the pleasures that surrounded him. Although he might have been despised and mocked, he was able to influence his family and lead them the right way. For this reason, he was favoured. God saw the need to preserve his life and that of those he was able to positively affect.

We can also stand out from the rest of the people in our schools by not going against the rules when everyone else has. Also, in our jobs by trying our hardest to give our best when other people do not see the need to. In our churches, by building each other up and not tearing people apart and in our communities by not abusing systems when everyone else does.

Thinking about crime and sexual perversion that goes on among our youth, one can choose to be different by not engaging in such acts. Also, in communities where there is wastage of the resources we have and messing up of our environment. We can stand out from the rest of the people by not following the multitude, in doing the wrong things.

As already mentioned, choosing to stand out is profoundly unpopular; this can cause us hurt and cost us in so many other ways. But should we choose to stand up for the right thing, we retain our reputation. We are also able to influence and lead others into a better way. Ultimately, we and those whose lives we have affected will be protected and preserved in perilous times.

Do you choose to stand out from the rest of the people or not?

CHAPTER QUESTIONS

&

THEMES FOR THOUGHT

- State two kinds of fear that can confront one who wants to standout?
- What could happen to us when we go along with the wrong things around us?
- Discuss the importance of standing out from the rest of the people?
- In which areas of life can we choose to stand out from the rest of the crowd?

YOU CAN SUMMARISE YOUR THOUGHTS

YOU CAN REVISIT YOUR THOUGHTS

CHAPTER 7

OBEDIENCE TO GOD

"So, Noah did everything as the Lord commanded him." (NLT)

Genesis 7:5

MESSAGE AND LEARNING

God is all knowing. He knows everything that happens now, much as he knows the things that are to come. He also knows the intents of the heart of men and where we will each end up should we follow these intentions. He therefore guides us based on his knowledge and love for us, and for everything he tells us, he has a reason. It is important therefore that we trust him to an extent of doing what he tells us to do. Knowing that, all instructions given to us by God are for our own benefit and by not obeying, will leave us miserable in this world.

In our obedience we show God how we love him. Also, people get to know we are his worshippers. We become blessed in all aspects of our lives when we are obedient. God draws us closer to him through our obedience and it makes us suitable candidates to be used by God to fulfil his plans and purposes. In all, we become blessed by God and are an example to others of how one can be blessed when we obey God.

An example of the benefit we get from obeying God is God's deliverance. This is presented in the passage when God saved Noah and his family from the flood, because he was the only person who obeyed God and did what pleased him. On the other hand, there are consequences for disobeying God. We only make situations worse for ourselves and do not get the benefit of obedience. Also, as seen in this chapter the wages of disobedience to God which the Christian bible calls sin, is death.

To be obedient means to agree with a set of instructions and thereby comply with them. In the passage, obedience is portrayed by Noah through his actions. Let us just take a quick look at some of the things God instructed him to do and his compliance towards his obedience.

Firstly, he was to build a boat. But this was not just an ordinary boat. It was one that had to be well built, in order to withstand the magnitude of a flood. This was going to wipe out all living creatures on the face of the earth except for a chosen few. But here is the situation, there was no rain at the time, neither was he living by the sea, but rather miles away from it. Yet, he went ahead to do as God had instructed. Noah built the boat according to God's specifications believing that if God created the water, then he alone knew the stresses and strains of the waves and which boat could withstand this. For instance, one might have thought using hard wood would have been more suitable. In the case where such a boat was to be built, as hard wood would be stronger, denser and more durable. However, God instructed him to use resinous wood and seal it with tar on the inside and out. We find out that resinous wood, although soft is easy to work with, has low density and its sap produces resin or a gum like residue. This might have made it easier for him to build the boat, promoted the boat's ability to float and enable it to stay securely together throughout the time of the flood. Additionally, the tar used had an extra benefit of preserving the wood against rot due to its water- repellent nature. God knew perfectly well, the material that could withstand such a flood and instructed him in that sense. Also, he had specifications in terms of how the boat was to measure. Building the boat using different specifications asides what God had commanded him, could have resulted in problems. Some of which could have been, it being too big and heavy causing it to sink or too small to contain them all.

Apart from the instructions given from God on how the boat was to be built, God told him to take seven pairs of each animal that he had approved for eating and for sacrifice, seven pairs each of every kind of bird and a pair of each of the other kinds to keep alive. Moreover, God's instructions to Noah to take more pairs of the approved animals for eating and sacrifice was to ensure there was enough of such kind to feed generations and also to be used for sacrifice. Of course, they would not have much need for the other animals and hence a pair each of them was sufficient to ensure their existence. Should Noah have disobeyed God by taking less of the approved animals, they sure would have run out of them and probably starved out of scarcity or gone extinct. Should he have taken more pairs of the other animals than needed, there would have been more of them than needed and may have caused the boat to sink.

Furthermore, he was also instructed to take enough food for his family and the animals. This was to ensure they had enough to sustain them for the duration. If Noah had taken less than was required both would have starved to death.

He also had to wait to be told by God when they had to enter and leave the boat. He saw the water drying up, yet he did not rush out of the boat. He waited until God instructed them to leave the boat before he let everyone off the boat. Just imagine what could have happened if they got out of the boat without the water receding. They would equally have drowned due to disobedience as the others did.

Imagine having been obedient through all the tough times and just when salvation is at hand, impatience causes us to miss out on the one thing that perfects salvation?

We learn from this chapter that, although God has the power to do all things, we see his power more clearly through our obedience to him. As through our obedience we submit to his will and plans for us, which is always the best. He does this by leading us on the right path. We in turn become obedient to God when we follow in the path he sets before us: when we follow in his ways exactly as we are commanded. This is obedience. But if we choose to ignore his ways or instructions and go on our own path, follow them partly or alter them in any way to suit us, we miss out on the rewards of obedience. We also learn that we might sometimes look foolish to others if we are to obey God, when the instructions he gives are incomprehensible to them. However, when we obey God, and do as we are told they later come to the realisation that God truly knows best and following in his instructions is always rewarding.

In summary, it is important for us to obey God for multiple reasons. One of which is that God knows what will happen in the future whilst we do not. God knows where we will each end up should we do the right or wrong thing.

Would you rather obey God or not?

CHAPTER QUESTIONS

&

THEMES FOR THOUGHT

- What can we benefit from God through our obedience to him?
- What are the consequences of disobedience to God?

YOU CAN SUMMARISE YOUR THOUGHTS

YOU CAN REVISIT YOUR THOUGHTS

CHAPTER 8

REAP WHAT YOU SOW

"As long as the earth endures, seedtime and harvest, cold and heat, summer and winter, day and night will never cease." (NIV)

Genesis 8: 22

MESSAGE AND LEARNING

We read in this chapter that, Noah's act of sacrifice unto God, resulted in God deciding never again to curse the earth. A good act has earned a good result- in essence, you reap what you sow. In addition to that, God further affirms his word, "as long as the earth remains, seedtime and harvest shall not cease". Firstly, God was no longer going to curse the earth again for man's sake, so the earth is to yield its strength to man once it is worked. Secondly, there shall always be a time to sow and a time to harvest if the earth remains. It stands therefore to reason that, each of us can harvest if we make the choice to sow. But then, our harvest will depend on the circumstances surrounding our sowing. The type of seed we sow, how much of it we sow, our attitude towards sowing, all determine our harvest.

Each of us will have to first identify our seeds and differentiate it from the fruit. Seeds are meant primarily for sowing and fruits for eating. However, if we choose to eat our fruit together with our seed and not sow it, then we will have nothing to look forward to come harvest time. It is those who can distinguish between the seed given them by God for sowing and the fruit meant for eating and likewise, go ahead to sow their seed, who always receive a harvest. But then, there are different types of seeds one can sow.

Choosing the right seeds to sow is also very important if we expect a good harvest. God has been so merciful to us that, for whatever harvest we expect, we can choose a seed of its kind to sow. If we expect to harvest apples, then we ought to sow apple seeds. We cannot sow tomato seeds and expect to harvest apples. We therefore must be mindful when it is seed time, of the type of seed we sow, bearing in mind that we shall surely reap a harvest of it. These can be seeds of our actions towards situations that befall us, the words we utter or our charitable gifts and for each of them we receive in kind a harvest of what has been sown. For instance, we will receive a harvest of poverty should we sow seeds of laziness. Similarly, if we speak unkind words, people will shun our company and we will end up reaping a harvest of loneliness. Seeds of impatience or hastiness gives a harvest of regrets. On the other hand, people who are charitable never run out of resources they freely gave as it has previously been sown. Also, sowing seeds of humility gives a harvest of upliftment. Here are some examples of good seeds we can sow in our time. Diligence, patience, hard work, and kindness. On the other hand, unforgiveness, bitterness, laziness are seeds we should be avoiding.

Many of us seem to forget, we harvest in multiples of what we sow. Also, should we expect to harvest more, then we should in fact be sowing a proportionate amount of what is been sown. From a different perspective, we will just be depriving ourselves of a great harvest should we decide to keep the seeds given to us by God and only choose to sow a small amount of them. I have come to realise that it is farmers who plan a great harvest who normally sow most of the seeds they have harvested in previous seasons. The more you reap, the more you sow. The more you expect to harvest, the more you ought to sow. It is all about having the right mentality to sow what you have in order to have a great harvest.

Finally, we ought to bear in mind that we will surely reap a harvest of what we have sown whether now or in the future considering different seeds have different times of harvest. All we need to do is wait for the right time to harvest. Bearing in mind that, seeds do not grow overnight and although we might reap within a short time after sowing some seeds, others might take longer to harvest. Hence, why we should not give up on a good seed and live in the hope of reaping a good harvest. Additionally, it is more reason why we should sow good seeds, so we can always be in the expectation of a good harvest. Similarly, avoiding the sowing of bad seeds for example theft, rudeness and wickedness will prevent us from living with the regrets of reaping a bad harvest.

Are the seeds you are sowing in your life good or bad? What would you want to harvest?

CHAPTER QUESTIONS

&

THEMES FOR THOUGHT

- What could happen if you choose to eat your seeds, as well as the fruit?
- Which farmer do you think will benefit more? One who saves more and sows less seeds, or the one who saves less and sows more seeds, considering both farmers have the same number of seeds, and all other conditions remain equal and favourable?

YOU CAN SUMMARISE YOUR THOUGHTS

YOU CAN REVISIT YOUR THOUGHTS

CHAPTER 9

RESPECTING BOUNDARIES

"One day he drank some wine he had made, and he became drunk and lay naked inside his tent. Ham, the father of Canaan, saw that his father was naked and went outside and told his brothers." (NLT)

Genesis 9:21-22

MESSAGE AND LEARNING

God in his wisdom set up boundaries since the time of creation. The sea respects its boundaries. However, if the sea ignores these boundaries and flows wherever it chooses to, the whole earth could be flooded. Also, man lives on land, birds in the air, and fish live in water and although all these are free to move to other habitats asides where they live, they know their boundaries and respect them. Should fish choose to live on land they will die in no time. Likewise, man can only stay in water but for a short period of time lest he too should die.

Boundaries form important aspects of our everyday lives, as they remind us of the extent to which we can go freely without trespassing on the grounds of others. In a way, they inform us of our limits and help prevent conflicts. They exit in diverse forms. Some of which are local and international boundaries, relational and cooperative boundaries. This chapter focuses on physical or territorial boundaries that exist in the home and considers areas where permission needs to be sought prior to entering. It partly considers relational boundaries to an extent. Asides our homes however, boundaries exist in our schools, workplaces and everyday lives and all these need to be respected.

Let's first consider some territorial boundaries that exist in our time. One of which is boundaries that exist at national levels. Every nation has its own boundaries and set of rules and regulations which should be abided by. Hence why, there is a need to find out about the requirements of a nation for which one is not a citizen and ensure all rules and regulations are followed prior to entering. This ensures laws governing crossing the national boundaries are respected and avoids the breaching of laws. It also prevents unnecessary punishments and penal encounters. Similarly, boundaries in the home need to be respected. Especially in situations where rooms have been assigned to individuals based on specific reasons. For instance, different rooms for males and females to allow them to understand their respective differences. Also, parents having separate rooms to their children so that they can enjoy some privacy retrospectively. I grew up learning the need to knock on my parent's door and waiting until I was told to enter, was a way of respecting boundaries and personal space. It is important to remember, if we share a room with someone it will be wise to respect their personal space and belongings. On the other hand, if we do not, then you should always knock out of respect before entering hence respecting the other person's boundaries.

Here is the case in which we read from this chapter of the bible of Ham not respecting his father's space and invading upon his privacy. In the first instance he crossed a boundary he should not have crossed without gaining permission. Also, he failed to respect and honour his father by not preserving his privacy but rather telling his brothers of their father's nakedness. Both physical and relational boundaries were breached in this instance. Physical in the sense that, he intruded upon his father's privacy without respecting it. Relational in that, he failed to honour his father. This resulted in Noah pronouncing a curse on Ham's descendants, Canaan, to be the lowest of servants to the descendants of Shem and Japheth and up until now the curse still stands.

We should endeavour to respect boundaries wherever we find ourselves. For instance, boundaries that exist between us and our superiors at work ought to be respected. Those we find between us and our teachers at school need also to be respected. We should also respect boundaries that exist between us and our colleagues remembering not to take for granted the relationship we have with each of these groups of people. Especially, when we find people in higher hierarchical groups, come down to our level to interact with us, we should still know our boundaries and respect them accordingly. This ensures we know the extent to which we can go in terms of our words and actions towards them and prevents conflicts and breakdowns in relationships.

In some cases, refusing to respect boundaries denies us of certain opportunities and favours, irritates or annoys the people whose boundaries we failed to respect, makes people shun our company, and as read in this chapter stops us from receiving what we should.

Would you make a choice to respect set boundaries?

CHAPTER QUESTIONS

&

THEMES FOR THOUGHT

- Discuss some examples of human boundaries that we are to respect?
- What measures would you put in place to help you respect these boundaries?
- How are you going to prove to your parents that you do respect their boundaries?

YOU CAN SUMMARISE YOUR THOUGHTS

YOU CAN REVISIT YOUR THOUGHTS

CHAPTER 10

BLESSINGS AND CURSES

"These are the clans that descended from Noah's sons, arranged by nation according to their lines of descent. All the nations of the earth descended from these clans after the great flood." (NLT)

Genesis 10:32

MESSAGE AND LEARNING

From Chapter 9 of the book of Genesis, we realise that we can make choices whether to earn blessings or receive curses in life. Both blessings and curses can be received directly from God, from a priest, from parents and from any other person. Seeing the goodness in his creation made God to pronounce blessings on all he created. However, God cursed man when he disobeyed him. Also, we read in the book of Numbers that, Aaron and his sons (who were priests) were to bless the people of Israel with special blessings after they had set themselves apart to the Lord in a special way. Likewise, Isaac in his old age asked his son Esau to prepare him a meal he loved in a way he liked it for him to eat, after which he would pronounce the blessings that belonged to him as a first born, before he died. Furthermore, when we do things for people and they are pleased with what we have done, they bless us.

Blessings follow a good act whereas a curse follows a bad act. God commanded the Israelites to keep the commandments so he would bless them and future generations. Whoever did not do so, would be punished, including generations to come. Therefore, through simple obedience, God gave them his blessings. Many a time, people say words of blessings into our lives when we have done something good to them or helped them in a particular way. Which also tells us that they should have been pleased with what we did for them, so as to speak words of blessings into our lives. One thing we must remember is that blessings do not come out of an angry heart but rather from a happy, cheerful or thankful heart. It is only happy people who bless! When you make someone happy, he blesses you. Much the same way, you could be cursed by a person to whom you have made angry. Curses can only work in our lives if there is a cause, so we should endeavour to do things in a way so as not to provoke a curse.

The blessings or curses we receive go a long way to affect our lives in many ways and can have lasting effects on us.

Women all over the world continue to experience painful birth as a result of Eve's dishonour to God and the subsequent curse pronounced on her by God. We also find out that until now, man must strive to survive.

We learnt from the previous chapter that Noah blessed the descendants of his two sons (Shem and Japheth) having honoured him while he pronounced a curse on the descendants of his son Ham, for dishonouring him. In this chapter, we realise that the blessings pronounced on Shem and Japheth's descendants and the curse pronounced on Ham's descendants still holds until this day. The Canaanites were serving the descendants of Shem and their territories were possessed by them following the curse pronounced on them by Noah.

Having gained knowledge of how we can either earn a blessing or curse, from whom we can earn it and its influence on our lives, it is vital therefore that we seek to act in a way to earn blessings and avoid curses.

Would you rather choose to earn a blessing upon you and your descendants or a curse?

CHAPTER QUESTIONS

&

THEMES FOR THOUGHT

- Can you name two things you are going to do from today in order to earn God's blessing.
- What are some of the things you can do for yourself to earn blessings from your parents?
- How can a blessing or curse work in our lives?

YOU CAN SUMMARISE YOUR THOUGHTS

YOU CAN REVISIT YOUR THOUGHTS

CHAPTER 11

UNITY

"Look!" he said. "The people are united, and they all speak the same language. After this, nothing they set out to do will be impossible for them!" (NLT)

Genesis 11:6

MESSAGE AND LEARNING

When people (family, church, friends, colleagues) are united, nothing they plan to do is impossible, that is if God allows it. People who are united, think alike, feel alike and express their thoughts and feelings in the same way, through words and actions. Such people live with the same purpose and this purpose gets accomplished because thoughts and feelings are the same and this drives what they do and how they do it. Additionally, more successful things are achieved when people are united, compared to what is achieved on an individual basis. This is because there is richness of ideas and skills when people are united. Also, decisions can easily be reached in a quicker way. In that, opinions are freely discussed, and each other's points of views respected, allowing for an agreed course of action to be taken.

Besides this, there is distribution of labour which makes workloads lighter and easier to accomplish. Unity gives more power, better security and defence. The opposite can be said of a group of people that are not united.

There are certain unique characteristics that can be identified within people who are united. One of these characteristics is a sense of belonging. We realise that people who are united get encouragement from the fact that, they belong to a group they can identify with. They are proud to be known as being part of that group. For that reason, they do all they possibly can to make the plans and purposes of the group into reality. People in a group that is united, also find comfort in the love that is demonstrated in the group. No one looks for ways to exploit or to take advantage of each other. Neither do people insist on their rights but rather see it as a privilege in benefiting from the group. As they individually identify themselves as one group pursuing a common purpose, this second characteristic of love is shown particularly through their act of selflessness. In that, they freely share whatever they have with others, care and show compassion to one another without holding back, because they see themselves as *one*. This makes a whole lot of difference in the sense that, a body which is healthy is WHOLE, that is ONE. Whereas we can easily identify a sick or weak body by stating which part is sick, be it head, hand or foot. Thereby, crippling the entire body as the identified part, thus can be a channel of destruction to the entire body. The fact that people can identify themselves as "one" body therefore makes it easier for them to be selfless in their acts and rule out selfishness. This makes all things possible as each person sees themselves as having a responsibility to make the body whole. A third characteristics is genuine humility, in that, no one in the group sees themselves as being better than anyone else. Everyone is equally valued, and contributions esteemed with importance. Hence, everyone willingly listens to suggestions and opinions of others without condemning. But, with an aim of making the best out of what has been contributed.

In addition to what has been discussed in the previous paragraph, there are things we can do on an individual basis to promote unity wherever we find ourselves. Some of which are having tolerance for one another, understanding and forgiving whoever offends us, respecting each other and staying committed.

This chapter presents to us people who were of one mind. Firstly, they sat down and came up with an idea, a thing of the mind to build a city with a tower that reaches to the skies. Secondly, they each felt the need, a thing of the heart to make a name for themselves. Finally, they each chose to build the city. This was a thing of the will so they will not be scattered abroad. For this reason, they were able to quickly put their efforts together and active progress was being achieved. Why, because they were united in mind, heart and will. In as much as, what they did displeased God, they were able to achieve what they started because they were united.

Are you planning on achieving a goal as a family, church, friends, colleagues etc? Then, the key to your success is Unity.

CHAPTER QUESTIONS

&

THEMES FOR THOUGHT

- What are some of the things you can do to promote unity in your family or wherever you find yourself?
- Identify some of the things that can cause friction and disunite a group of people?
- Do you believe people who are united share a common purpose? If so, why?
- State and explain 3 characteristics that can be identified with people who are united.
- What are your thoughts concerning united people and success?

YOU CAN SUMMARISE YOUR THOUGHTS

YOU CAN REVISIT YOUR THOUGHTS

CHAPTER 12

SEPARATION

Then the Lord said to Abram, "Leave your country, your relatives and your father's family. Go to the land I will show you. I will make you a great nation, and I will bless you. I will make you famous. And you will be a blessing to others. I will bless those who bless you. I will place a curse on those who harm you. And all the people on earth will be blessed through you." (ICB)

Genesis 12:1-3

MESSAGE AND LEARNING

Sometimes, God will want us to set ourselves apart from certain things, places or be alone away from the things that can hinder his fellowship with us. This leaves us entirely for his use, in that we are free from the very things that distract us and cause us to miss out on his blessings. Setting ourselves apart for God, helps us to stay holy as we do all we can to keep in close fellowship with him. We are also able to hear much clearer from God when he speaks to us in this way. Besides this, we concentrate much better on his guidance without losing focus, which leads us to the blessings he has proposed for us. More so, we find ourselves out of reach of the things or company that can change our course. Stopping us from receiving from God, thereby allowing for his blessings to manifest in our lives. Furthermore, God can use us to accomplish his purpose when we set ourselves apart for his use.

We find in our scripture reading that, Abraham (who was previously called Abram) was faced with a choice of whether to separate himself from his country, relatives, and father's house, and go to a land God was going to show him. He had to leave his father's house because it was a place of idol worship. He had to take that step of faith leaving the place he had lived all his life, the things he enjoyed doing in that place and the company of people that surrounded him to go to a place unknown to him. This must have been a difficult choice for him at the time, yet he set himself apart for God. In the same way, God would sometimes want us to separate ourselves from certain company we enjoy (particularly if this is a bad one), things we find pleasure in (for instance watching television) or even denying ourselves of certain foods for a time so he can have our sole attention in the time he shares with us.

As a result of Abraham's choice of separating himself from the things God told him to, he was blessed by God, made famous, became a blessing to others, his nation and the entire world. Likewise, we also will be blessed by God, if we choose to separate ourselves from the things God has asked us to do.

Will you be willing to set yourself apart for God, should there be a need to do so?

CHAPTER QUESTIONS

&

THEMES FOR THOUGHT

- What are some of the things God would want you to separate yourself from?
- Why do you think it is necessary to separate yourself from these things?
- List all the blessing God promised Abraham in this chapter when he told him to separate himself.

YOU CAN SUMMARISE YOUR THOUGHTS

YOU CAN REVISIT YOUR THOUGHTS

CHAPTER 13

CHOICE BY FLESH OR FAITH

"Lot looked around and saw that the whole plain of Jordan toward Zoar was well watered, like the garden of the Lord, like the land of Egypt. (This was before the Lord destroyed Sodom and Gomorrah.) So, Lot chose for himself the whole plain of Jordan and set out toward the East. The two men parted company." (NIV)

Genesis 13:10&11

MESSAGE AND LEARNING

The things we see, hear, smell, taste and touch influence the choices we make. We can, however, make choices by following the lead of God and not by receiving information from our physical senses alone. Choices made by receiving information from our physical senses are made under the influence of the flesh and those made by the lead of God are made by faith. We are, most of the time led into making choices under the influence of the flesh and not by faith as there is no physical evidence of what to expect in the moment when choices are made by faith. Choices made by faith in God, require our understanding that God exists. If we believe he exists, then we can personally relate to him, in that, he can talk to us. This also means that we can act on his word: that is to do what he says even if we do not know what to expect. That is faith, acting on the word of God not just for now but all the time. This could be by acting on the spoken word of God, given directly to us by his spirit or by the written word of God which we read from the Christian bible.

In the scripture reading, we find out that both Abraham and Lot had to make choices of where to live when they had to part company, as the land, they settled on could not support both of them and their possessions. Lot made a choice based on the well-watered plain he saw in the valley of Jordan toward Zoar. Although, this part of the land was appealing to the eyes as it was well watered and fertile, it was a corrupt land. The people who lived there were usually wicked and sinned greatly against the Lord and it was in God's plan to destroy it. By using our physical senses, we would most certainly agree it was the best land to live on. But then, this is a choice based on the influence of the flesh as he was led into making the choice solely by what he saw. On the other hand, Abraham's choice was as a result of the lead of God. The land was not one that would appeal to anyone. It did not look physically attractive in anyway. He acted on what God said and did as he was told. This is a choice made by faith, acting on the word of God no matter what the cost and trusting that he will never let you down.

Lot walked by sight, and he ended up in trouble. He did not get to permanently possess the land he chose to live on. Also, he lost everything he laboured to obtain and his wife as well. He was separated from God and ended up committing the sin of incest. However, as Abraham was led into making a choice based on the lead of God, that is a choice by faith, he and his descendants got to possess the land and were blessed by God through this very choice.

When we read further in the latter chapters, we will realise that choices we make based on the lead of the flesh are not always what they turn out to be. It may look attractive on the outside, but does this reflect what it is on the inside? It may taste sweet but is it good for your health? It may seem to be the best using the physical senses but is that what it really is? We learn choices made by faith are rewarding as God never gives us the worst but the best of things, even though they may not reflect the way we expect them to, now.

Are the choices we make in our daily lives (that is what we do, who we give to, what we eat, where we live). based on flesh or faith?

CHAPTER QUESTIONS

&

THEMES FOR THOUGHT

- List three choices you are not going to make from now onwards by the flesh.
- List three choices you are going to make from now onwards by faith.

YOU CAN SUMMARISE YOUR THOUGHTS

YOU CAN REVISIT YOUR THOUGHTS

CHAPTER 14

HELPING OTHERS

"When Abram heard that his relative had been taken captive, he called out the three hundred and eighteen trained men born in his household and went in pursuit as far as Dan. During the night Abram divided his men to attack them and he routed them, pursuing them as far as Hobah, north of Damascus. He recovered all the goods and brought back his relative Lot and his possessions, together with the women and the other people".

Genesis 14: 14-16

MESSAGE AND LEARNING

We can offer help to family, friends, neighbours or even strangers. The help we give others can be in the form of money, time, energy, attention or ideas. No matter how big or small the help we give is, it can go a long way to meet a need in another person's life.

Helping others also makes us better in a way. It can make us feel happy, fulfilled, rewarded and empowered. Apart from this, when we help others, it opens more opportunities for us to gain more out of the help we have given. For example, when we help someone by explaining things to them, our understanding of that thing is increased as compared to what we previously had before we offered the help. Jesus said we should give, and we shall in turn receive a measure that far outweighs what we have given.

We read in this chapter that when Abraham heard his nephew Lot was captured, he was concerned for his wellbeing. He was motivated to do all he could in his power to help him. For this reason, God in turn offered him his help. Abraham had to help his nephew Lot, who had been captured by the four kings of Elam, Goiim, Babylonia and Ellasar. These kings had previously fought against the five kings (of Sodom, Gomorrah, Admah, Zeboiim and Bela) and took all their food and wealth including Lot, Abraham's nephew who lived in Sodom with them. The four king's army must have been powerful to be able to have defeated the five king's army. To be able to rescue his nephew therefore, Abraham needed to have a bigger and stronger army to defeat the four king's army. The bible tells us Abraham called together the three hundred and eighteen fighting men in his camp who were able to pursue and conquer the four king's army.

Abraham's small three hundred and eighteen army compared to the four king's strong army realistically did not stand a chance of defeating the four king's army. However, the bible tells us that, Abraham's army was able to defeat them, and they brought back his nephew Lot, his possessions, the other prisoners and their possessions. For his reward the king of Sodom and king of Salem met him upon his return.

He received a blessing from the king of Salem, who was also a priest of God by name of Melchizedek as a reward. The king went even further to offer Abraham everything he recovered. But Abraham refused to accept them as he did not want to benefit from someone else's misfortune. Hence, the whole concept of this chapter in helping others.

We learn that Abraham could only have rescued them from this strong army with the help of God. This teaches us that, whenever we make up our mind to help others, we receive God's help. It does not matter what we have or how strong we are, if we decide to help others. What matters is our willingness to help them.

We must remember that, if we refuse to help others when we can, God can always raise other people to help them. When this happens, we miss out on the blessings attached to the help we should have offered. Also, we might find it difficult to ask for their help in times of our greatest need when they are in a better position to help us.

Will you be willing to help someone in need or not? What choice will you make when it comes to offering help to others?

CHAPTER QUESTIONS

&

THEMES FOR THOUGHT

- Do you remember a time you could have helped someone but refused to? If you were faced with the same situation now, would you make the same choice? If yes, why, if no, why?
- Has there ever been a time in your life when you helped someone in need. How did you feel after offering them the help? How did they feel having received your help?
- Have you ever received help from anyone before? What were your thoughts after receiving the help? What do you think could have been different should you not have received the help?
- What kind of help would you offer your family moving forwards?
- In what ways will helping others make you a better person?

YOU CAN SUMMARISE YOUR THOUGHTS

YOU CAN REVISIT YOUR THOUGHTS

CHAPTER 15

TO BE HOPEFUL

Then the LORD said to him, "No, your servant will not be your heir, for you will have a son of your own who will be your heir."(NLT)
Genesis 15: 1

MESSAGE AND LEARNING

Hope, as defined in the Oxford dictionary is a feeling of expectation and desire for a particular thing to happen. When we have something to hope for, we are motivated to work hard believing we can make things happen. We can be hopeful to achieve our desires in life, for instance, career, marriage and family and therefore do what we can to make these things happen. In this way, hope enables us to achieve set goals in life. Hope gives us the joy that keeps us going and helps us through tough times. On the other hand, when we have nothing to hope for, we get discouraged, we could give up easily when faced with challenges and could miss out on many opportunities and blessings in life. Also, we end up effortless in the things we do and so, do not achieve the desired results. More so, we end up achieving less in life.

God in his love has made available many promises in his word to us that can give us hope. By trusting in his word, we become hopeful of receiving all his promises. For instance, Jesus promises us in the book of John he is going to prepare a place for us in his father's house. This gives us something to hope for knowing that if we love God and remain in him, we will get to live with him forever and more so in this new place he is going to prepare for us. Furthermore, we are motivated by the hope we have from this promise to do our possible best to get to live in this place someday. In a way, the hope we have, also helps us endure all things while looking forward to the joy and rewards of living in the place we hope to live.

The bible also promises us that all may go well with us and that we may live a long and prosperous life should we obey our parents. When we are hopeful to live long and have all things go well, we do our best then to obey our parents.

Abraham had nothing to hope for initially, but God gave him something to hope for, something he could look forward to. Having no heir of his own, made him reluctant to accept God's blessings. After all, one of his slaves would have been his heir and there was no reason why a master will accumulate wealth for a slave.

Generally speaking, heirs are children, descendants or other close relatives rather than slaves. His sense of hope was as a result of God's promise to bless him with a son. This promise made him hopeful. He trusted in God's promise and the hope of having a son who will be an heir to him, gave him the joy to endure all things until he bore his son, Isaac.

We can also be hopeful by having confidence in the character of God, that is by believing in the fact that he is good, does not tell a lie and does what he says. As well as that, we can believe in the promises of God and not focus on the present unpleasant circumstances we are faced with but rather be in expectation of the good things to come. In this way we live in hope by seeing beyond the present suffering while thinking about the joys ahead of us.

Do you choose to live in hope or not?

CHAPTER QUESTIONS

&

THEMES FOR THOUGHT

- Name one of God's promises that gives you hope?
- Finding hope in this promise, how will it make you act differently to achieve the promise?
- What are your expectations should you work toward achieving the promise?
- What could happen if you had not had this promise of hope?

YOU CAN SUMMARISE YOUR THOUGHTS

YOU CAN REVISIT YOUR THOUGHTS

CHAPTER 16

SELF HELP OR GOD'S HELP

Now Sarai, Abram's wife, had borne him no children. But she had an Egyptian slave named Hagar; so, she said to Abram, "The Lord has kept me from having children. Go, sleep with my slave; perhaps I can build a family through her." (NIV)

Genesis 16: 1&2

MESSAGE AND LEARNING

Sometimes we are faced with situations in life in which we feel we can do things on our own or make what God has said concerning our lives happen without God's help. We forget our own strength, knowledge and abilities can fail us and that all help comes from God. If we have amassed wealth, it is God who gave us the power to make wealth. If we have a successful career or business, it is God who allowed it to happen.

God promised Abraham he was going to bless him with a son but instead of waiting for the promise to come into reality, Abraham decided to help himself by sleeping with and impregnating his servant Hagar to fulfil the promise. Meanwhile, God had promised to give Abraham the son not by Hagar or any other woman but by Sarah (who was previously called Sarai), his wife. The son God promised him was going to be Abraham's heir and the promise was made specifically to Abraham and Sarah. However, having waited for some time for the promise of a son and not see it happening, they tried to make the promise of God happen on their own. Instead of allowing God to help them the way he knew best, they chose to do it their own way. Abraham heeded to Sarah's suggestion to sleep with Hagar, so that through her, she could have children. However, this choice was in no way going to help them fulfil God's promise to them nor give them the satisfaction they longed for. Rather, it paved way for troubles, regrets and hurt.

One way in which the devil deceives us to self-help instead of waiting for God's help, is when the time for God's promise to happen in our lives is not yet due and the devil deceives us in a way as to think it is being delayed. In this way, it causes us to think we can make things happen for ourselves. Other times, the people around us might suggest ways to us to self-help. The point is, some of the advice given to us by these people might sound appealing and seem a good way to help ourselves. But not all advice that seems to be good is of God and can help us in these situations. Moreover, we realise helping ourselves leads to many troubles and leaves us in a worse state than we previously were. We entangle ourselves with many more problems when we self-help instead of waiting for God's help.

We find out from this passage that the act of self-help brought a lot of problems into Abraham's family. Firstly, we are told Hagar treated her mistress Sarah with contempt when she knew she was pregnant. Also, Sarah felt despised by Hagar which made her unhappy. Further to this, Sarah blamed Abraham for the challenges that the family faced, making him give her permission to deal with Hagar as she saw fit. Sarah in turn treated Hagar so harshly, to the extent that she ran away.

In all, there was a passing of blame and friction in Abraham and Sarah's marriage and a breakdown in family relationships. Abraham had two sons, the illegitimate son with the slave Hagar (Ishmael) and the promised son (Isaac) with his wife Sarah. This act of self-help produced two blood lines. The Israelites come from the blood line of Isaac and the Arabs from the blood line of Ishmael. Still to this day, there are troubles in the Middle East due to the friction that still exists between the family blood lines.

Instead of self-helping and living with regrets, we can make a choice of asking for God's help through prayer. When we are faced with challenging situations we can also, trust in the character of God, knowing that he is a good God, always doing what is good. In this way we are assured that God will fulfil all the promises he has made to us. We need to be patient and rely on God as he always does things when he feels the time is right.

Would you self-help or rather allow God to help you?

CHAPTER QUESTIONS

&

THEMES FOR THOUGHT

- What causes people to decide to choose self-help over God's help?
- What are the consequences that befell Abraham's family when he chose to help himself instead of depending on God?
- Upon knowing what happened to Abraham, would you still allow the devil to deceive you into helping yourself? Why?

YOU CAN SUMMARISE YOUR THOUGHTS

YOU CAN REVISIT YOUR THOUGHTS

CHAPTER 17

CIRCUMCISION/ CUTTING OFF OLD LIFE

"This is the covenant that you and your descendants must keep: Each male among you must be circumcised. You must cut off the flesh of your foreskin as a sign of the covenant between me and you." (NLT)

Genesis 17: 10 &11

MESSAGE AND LEARNING

To circumcise literally means to cut around. Two kinds of circumcision are presented in the Christian bible. Physical circumcision and spiritual circumcision.

Physical circumcision as practiced in the Old Testament, was a seal of God's covenant with Abraham and was an outward act that signified the removal of the needless carnal desires of the flesh. In a way, it symbolised the purification of the heart or the cutting away of oneself from all wrong doings or sinful acts which in bible terms, is spiritual circumcision. It also, represented a seal of righteousness that comes through faith. In that, by performing this act, a person confirms their faith in God with a visible proof of having put an end to their previous sinful life. Till this day, Jews practice the physical act of circumcision in which the foreskin of a male is surgically removed.

The choice in this chapter is not about the physical act of circumcision but rather the spiritual concept of circumcision.

We gather from this chapter that God wanted to enter into a covenant with the people of Israel. He wanted to be their God and to bless them so other nations will know how God can bless his people; those who obey him. He was going to play his part in the covenant by making them a multitude of nations. They will be a mighty nation and kings will be among them. This was going to be an everlasting covenant between Israel and generations to come. However, it required the people of Israel to be circumcised. They had to cut themselves off from the old lives they lived: the very sinful lives everyone else lived which upset God. All links they had with the former master of their lives which made them gratify the desires of the flesh had to be cut off so they could receive new birth by the spirit of God. Then, they will have a new name. They could bear God's name and will be children of God and be set apart for him. Although, it was required for them to physically circumcise each male, obeying such a simple act showed their willingness to obey God's commands, as children of God and hence receive from him as children receive from a father. It was a physical act but as already stated proved their faith in God.

The human heart is a gateway to all the choices we make and the actions we take in life. It serves as a link between our senses (what we see, hear, feel, smell and taste) and the choices we make. We desire with our hearts the things we see, hear, feel, smell and taste and this guides our will to say or do the things we do every day of our lives. By serving as a gateway, the heart can allow both good and bad situations access to our will and influence the choices we make. An uncircumcised heart, however, desires, gives access to, harbours and bears unclean acts which the Christian bible calls acts of the flesh. Examples of these are sexual immorality, impurity and debauchery, idolatry and witchcraft, hatred, discord, jealousy, fits of rage, selfish ambition, dissensions, factions and envy, drunkenness, orgies and the like. When these acts are allowed to function in a person's life, it prevents them from receiving God's goodness. It also brings shame on a person and leads to separation from God and death.

However, by choosing to circumcise our hearts, we gratify the desires of the spirit. In that, we desire, allow, harbour and bear fruits of the spirit (love, joy, peace, patience, kindness, goodness, gentleness, faithfulness and self-control). This glorifies God and makes way for the blessings of God and his purpose to be fulfilled in our lives.

Unfortunately, the bible makes us aware that each one of us is sinful from birth and that our imaginations are continually evil from birth. But then, if we cut the links we have with our old sinful nature and allow God to start all over again with us, thus making us into the people he wants us to be and not the people we want to be, then we too can be called his children.

Until we part company with the desires of the world, we cannot enjoy all the good things God has planned for us. This can be done through repentance with an inward and outward evidence of separation from the desires of the flesh. In that, we assess our lives and conclude that we have not lived the way God intended us to. Also, we have lots of bad ways linked to our lives from the past which if not cut off can destroy our lives and rid us of many of God's blessings. Thus, we decide to live our lives moving forward in the way God wants us to and not gratify the desires of the flesh. Moving forwards, we can put these thoughts into actions. When we do this, God can enter into a covenant with us. Then we too can live in line with God's perfect will and be fulfilled in life.

Will you take the necessary steps required for you to be spiritually circumcised so you can receive the entire blessings God has in store for you?

CHAPTER QUESTIONS

&

THEMES FOR THOUGHT

- How do you understand the term circumcision in the bible?
- Why did God give Abraham the ceremony of circumcision?
- How would you apply the concept of circumcision into your daily life?

YOU CAN SUMMARISE YOUR THOUGHTS

YOU CAN REVISIT YOUR THOUGHTS

CHAPTER 18

SHOWING HOSPITALITY

"The Lord appeared to Abraham near the great trees of Mamre while he was sitting at the entrance to his tent in the heat of the day. Abraham looked up and saw three men standing nearby. When he saw them, he hurried from the entrance of his tent to meet them and bowed low to the ground." (NIV)

Genesis 18:1- 2

MESSAGE AND LEARNING

Hospitality is the friendly and generous reception and entertainment of guests, visitors or strangers. It is a way of showing love for strangers or people we do not know. We can be hospitable to people who are new to our class, school, church, neighbourhood, community or workspace. The book of Hebrews of the Christian bible encourages us not to neglect to show hospitality to strangers, as by doing so others have entertained angles unawares. By showing hospitality you can be blessed in many ways.

Three lessons can be learnt from Abraham's act of showing hospitality.

Firstly, we are to take the initiative to show hospitality and not wait for people to ask for help when we know they will benefit from our help. Having identified someone who needs to be shown hospitality, we can extend whatever help we can, without them having to ask for it. The word of God encourages us to continue to remember those in prison as if we were together with them in prison, and those who are mistreated as if we ourselves were suffering. The key word in this instance is 'remember'. When we are able to bring to mind an awareness of someone or a situation that needs an intervention, then we are more likely to be in a position to help. This part of scripture also teaches us to put ourselves in the same situation these people are in. By doing so, we are more likely to be hospitable to them knowing we would not want to go through the same situations that they are going through. It will enable us to think about what help we might need to give, if we were in the same position and be able to help them better. We should also bear in mind that, many people would for one reason or another, not want to approach us when they actually need our help. It could be for fear that they may be mocked if they asked for our help. Also, they may not ask for our help due to the shame of the situation they are in, not being capable of helping themselves or the fear of being bothersome to others.

Seeing the visitors from afar, Abraham hurriedly went to meet up with them and offered to help them. He did not wait for them to come and ask for his help. He thought about them from afar. He remembered them from a distance. He knew they had travelled a long way and would need their feet washed as per custom. He also encouraged them to rest and have something to eat and drink.

We see around us many who we could extend our hospitality to. But the thing is, do we approach them and offer our help? Or do we forget about them and wait for them to ask us for help? In their asking, are we even willing to help?

The second lesson from Abraham's act of hospitality is to have the right attitude when showing hospitality to others. The word of God tells us to offer hospitality to one another without grumbling. Additionally, it encourages us to give what we have decided in our heart to give, not reluctantly or under compulsion, for God loves a cheerful giver. When we use the right attitude when showing hospitality to others, it makes them happier to receive what we have to offer them. Also, God will generously provide all we need. This way, we will always have everything we require with plenty left over to share with others. Abraham was quick to help. He asked Sarah to get three large measures of the best flour, asked a servant to select a tender calf and prepare it. Furthermore, Abraham waited on them whilst they ate. This tells us how, willing, eager, cheerful, patient, kind, understanding, selfless and humble he was in his act of showing hospitality to the three visitors.

Thirdly, we are to think about it as though we are doing it for God when showing hospitality. For in fact, whatever we do for others, we do for the Lord. This will help make it easier to do what we must do. The scripture below throws more light on this:

Matthew 25:31-46 "When the Son of Man comes in his glory, and all the angels with him, he will sit on his glorious throne. All the nations will be gathered before him, and he will separate the people one from another as a shepherd separates the sheep from the goats. He will put the sheep on his right and the goats on his left. "Then the King will say to those on his right, 'Come, you who are blessed by my Father; take your inheritance, the kingdom prepared for you since the creation of the world. For I was hungry, and you gave me something to eat, I was thirsty, and you gave me something to drink, I was a stranger and you invited me in, I needed clothes and you clothed me, I was sick, and you looked after me, I was in prison and you came to visit me.'

"Then the righteous will answer him, 'Lord, when did we see you hungry and feed you, or thirsty and give you something to drink? When did we see you a stranger and invite you in, or needing clothes and clothe you? When did we see you sick or in prison and go to visit you?' "The King will reply, 'Truly I tell you, whatever you did for one of the least of these brothers and sisters of mine, you did for me.'

We learn from this chapter that Abraham's act of offering hospitality opened a wealth of opportunities for him.

Firstly, Sarah was going to bear a son in a year's time, meaning Abraham will have an heir when in fact we know it is impossible due to their ages.

Secondly, God made known his plans to him. He told Abraham, that he was going to destroy Sodom and Gomorrah due to their sinful acts.

Finally, he found favour in the sight of God, in that God granted Abraham's request of not destroying Sodom and Gomorrah if he was to find righteous men.

We too, by showing hospitality to others, can find favour with God and men, have our requests granted and most importantly help others with their needs.

Will you be willing to show hospitality to others as led by God?

CHAPTER QUESTIONS

&

THEMES FOR THOUGHT

- Give an example of a situation whereby you can offer hospitality to someone?
- What do you think is the best way to offer hospitality?

YOU CAN SUMMARISE YOUR THOUGHTS

YOU CAN REVISIT YOUR THOUGHTS

CHAPTER 19

TO LOOK BACK OR NOT

"Flee for your lives," the angels told him. "And don't look back. Escape to the mountains. Don't stay down here on the plain or you will die." (TLB)

Genesis 19: 17

MESSAGE AND LEARNING

Why would anyone want to stay or return to a place of destruction when they had been offered a safer place to flee to which offers a better standard of life than they had previously? Why would anyone prefer to go back to a past lifestyle, circumstance or habit that ruined their joy, peace and comfort when they had been offered a safer existence? To look back in this sense means to have a longing in our heart and minds for the life, things and pleasures we have left behind bearing in mind that it ruined our previous lives. When we desire again, yearn for or ponder upon the things we have left behind with a longing for them, we are looking back.

In our reading, we find out that Sodom and Gomorrah were sinful cities. The people who lived there did wrong in the sight of God and were not willing to repent. God had been patient with them for a long time in his expectations that they will change their ways, but they did not. When God had simply had enough of their wickedness, he sent two angels to go and destroy the place. He, however, did not want Lot and his family who lived a righteous life to be destroyed with the wicked people who live there. Do you remember a time in the bible when God destroyed the wicked but spared the righteous? So, the angels therefore told Lot to flee the city together with his wife and two daughters before it was destroyed, lest they too will be destroyed. The instructions given to them were clearly to run for their lives, not to stop anywhere in the valley and not to look back, lest they too will die.

God in his mercies always delivers the righteous from situations that oppress them and torment their righteous souls. However, when God saves us from a life that did not benefit us in the past, he does not want us to long for it again. It could be that we would have left possessions, relationships and things that gave us pleasure behind whilst we journeyed into the unknown, just us Lot did with his family. But he wants us to trust him. He wills for us to trust his lead to move us from the valley (our low estate) to the mountains (our uplifting). There may be discouragement along the way and circumstances that may try to stop us on the way, but we are encouraged not to stop anywhere in the valley. As long as we have not been completely delivered from the valley to the mountains, from our situation of distress in the past to comfort in the future, we are to keep going until we reach the top. More so, we are never to look back. Thus, look forwards to the future, not backwards to the past.

Lot's wife, however, looked back. In her case, looking back meant she had a longing for life back in Sodom and Gomorrah and therefore a longing for the sinful life there. For this reason, she turned into a pillar of salt. She was destroyed and did not get to her destination.

We should remember however that, looking back at the things which used to ruin us but from which we have been delivered, can lead to our destruction. Also, that, God is in the process of saving us from the evils of the world and the destruction that Jesus has said is coming upon the world. Just as Lot's wife had started fleeing the sinful city for a better place, yet did not get to her destination, we too can turn back and be destroyed, not get what has been promised to us or miss out on better opportunities if we turn back to the very things that had destroyed us in the past. The Christian bible advises us to remember Lot's wife and not turn back to the things that destroy our lives.

Do you intend to look back or not?

CHAPTER QUESTIONS

&

THEMES FOR THOUGHT

- Think about the things God has saved you from? A place, friends, hobbies, habit, character or conduct.
- Why is it important not to look back at these former situations?

YOU CAN SUMMARISE YOUR THOUGHTS

YOU CAN REVISIT YOUR THOUGHTS

CHAPTER 20

MAINTAINING INTEGRITY

"Abraham moved south to the Negev and lived for a while between Kadesh and Shur, and then he moved on to Gerar. While living there as a foreigner, Abraham introduced his wife, Sarah, by saying, "She is my sister." So, King Abimelech of Gerar sent for Sarah and had her brought to him at his palace. (NLT)

Genesis 20:1- 2

MESSAGE AND LEARNING

When a person has integrity, they are true to themselves and do the right thing in all circumstances even if no one is watching them. They have strong morals and ethical principles such as being truthful, honest, free of deceit no matter the challenges they face, are responsible and respectable, not compromising their morals and principles.

This chapter teaches us that we should endeavour to walk in integrity no matter the situation that befalls us. When we do this, we are maintaining our integrity. We sometimes find out that we are tempted to compromise our integrity at certain points of our lives. Factors such as, the fear of the unknown, losing something or someone and wanting to achieve our desires can cause us to compromise our integrity. But, when we compromise our integrity, we can end up in shame, live with regret and lose the trust others have in us. We could also get ourselves into more trouble than before and cause trouble for others. Furthermore, it shows our lack of faith in God.

Let us consider a child who always gets top grades in his class. He will be loved and respected by the people around him. If for some reason, this child for fear of losing his place as top of the class chooses to cheat in a test and is caught, no one will have faith in him anymore. He will lose the trust people had in him. Some might even think he had always been cheating the whole time to get the grades he had, even though it may have been the only time he cheated. He could also end up getting punished for this act.

Abraham was a man of integrity but chose to compromise his integrity for fear of losing his life. He told a lie. He falsely declared Sarah as not being his wife. He was not being truthful in his actions. He compromised these actions in order to have his own way over the situation he was in. He did not want to lose his life because of Sarah neither did he want to lose Sarah as a wife to another man. However, by not maintaining his integrity, he could have been punished by the king, had God not intervened. Also, but for God's intervention and mercy, the king would have been punished by God because of Abraham's actions (as he would have taken another man's wife).

Although it can be difficult in some situations to maintain one's integrity, doing so earns us trust and respect and opens doors of opportunities for us and leaves us happy.

Would you always do the right thing or not? If yes, do you choose to maintain your integrity?

CHAPTER QUESTIONS

&

THEMES FOR THOUGHT

- Name one thing that can tempt us or cause us to compromise our integrity?
- Why did Abraham compromise his integrity?
- What could have happened to him after compromising his integrity had God not intervened?
- Can you name one person in the bible who maintained his integrity asides Jesus? In what way did he/she do this?

YOU CAN SUMMARISE YOUR THOUGHTS

YOU CAN REVISIT YOUR THOUGHTS

CHAPTER 21

PATIENCE/ IMPATIENCE

"Now the Lord was gracious to Sarah as he had said, and the Lord did for Sarah what he had promised. Sarah became pregnant and bore a son to Abraham in his old age, at the very time God had promised him." (NIV)

Genesis 21:1-2

MESSAGE AND LEARNING

In bible terms, we are patient when we wait expectantly for a promise to be fulfilled. Patience reveals our faith in God's timings.

When God called Abraham, father of the Jews, he promised to make him a great nation. Through Abraham's descendants, God was going to bless nations on the earth. But Abraham had no child and both he and Sarah, his wife were ageing. Through the years, God continued to remind Abraham of his promise. This meant years of waiting patiently for the promise to be fulfilled. It got to a point in time however, when both Abraham and Sarah could no longer wait for the promised child.

Their actions of impatience resulted in the birth of Ishmael to Abraham and Hagar.

When God's appointed time finally came, Isaac was born to Abraham and Sarah as promised by God. This should have resulted in endless joy as they had waited a long time to have him but because of their act of impatience along the way, the joy they had was cut short. They had rushed into getting Ishmael who was not the promised child and later realised they did not need him anymore. More so, Ishmael and his mother Hagar, made fun of Isaac which upset Sarah and for that reason they had to get rid of both Hagar and Ishmael. An act of impatience had resulted in regrets, blame, suffering and breakdown in relationships.

In our time, many find it difficult to wait for the right time. Some rush to find jobs before pursuing their careers and after working so long and having their lives entangled in other responsibilities, later realise they should embark on a career. But then, having left it far too long than they should have, struggle through pursuing the chosen career. Others rush into premarital affairs without being patient and preparing for marriage. The majority of these people find themselves regretting this decision as they contract venereal diseases, have unplanned pregnancies or end up marrying the wrong partner as a result of their impatience.

We later realise we do not really need what we rush to get if we are not patient to wait for God's promises and timings. Sooner have we received the things we rush for; do we want to get rid of them. Other times, the things we are in haste to get creates problems into our lives which brings us misery. Remember all good and perfect gifts comes from above. Most certainly, we realise God's promises and plans for our lives are the best for us and happen at the right time. The time, he knows we will make the most out of what is given to us. To cherish it and have endless joy once we receive it. If we are to wait for his timings, we will find out they are well worth waiting for.

Would you rather wait for God's promise and appointed time or rush into getting things for yourself?

CHAPTER QUESTIONS

&

THEMES FOR THOUGHT

- Have you ever been impatient with someone or with God? Can you explain what happened prior to you getting impatient, during the time of your impatience and the after-effects?
- Would you now be patient with God or not, and why?

YOU CAN SUMMARISE YOUR THOUGHTS

YOU CAN REVISIT YOUR THOUGHTS

CHAPTER 22

PASSING GOD'S TEST

"This is what the Lord says: Because you have obeyed me and have not withheld even your son, your only son, I swear by my own name that I will certainly bless you. I will multiply your descendants beyond number, like the stars in the sky and the sand on the seashore. Your descendants will conquer the cities of their enemies. And through your descendants all the nations of the earth will be blessed—all because you have obeyed me." (NLT)

Genesis 22:16-18

MESSAGE AND LEARNING

Abraham had to pass God's test of faith and obedience. He was to sacrifice the son through whom God was going to bless him and for whom he had waited so long for. Take note of the fact that God wanted him to sacrifice the seed through which he was going to be blessed. Unless he was sacrificed, he would abide alone. This does not seem like an easy test to take. Should he have been told the reward prior to taking the test, it would still have been very challenging. In the sense that, he had waited so long a time to get Isaac, loved him and would not want to lose him even if he was promised more children by God. God has many wonderful promises for us in the bible, but they all come with conditions. There are things we must do to receive these promises. If you give, you will receive far more than you have given. When you forgive others the wrongs they do to you, the many wrongs you have done to others will be forgiven. We know all these promises but how often have we passed the test of giving to receive?

I cannot remember ever taking an easy test in life. Although, I have at times achieved great results while schooling, they have been particularly challenging. My greatest achievements came with adequate preparation, understanding of the questions, following the instructions given and staying focused with an aim of doing nothing but my best.

Life is full of tests, hence, why we should always be prepared and aim to pass the test of life. To do well in a test, one will need to prepare adequately for it. It could mean you have to know the kind of test you are taking, its requirements, the amount of effort you need to put into it and the results you would like to achieve at the end of it. So, if you are to take a test in Mathematics for instance, you need to know if you would be required to use a calculator or not. This will guide you into knowing how much effort to put into your learning. If you want to achieve a high mark, you should prepare well in advance.

Abraham got up early the next morning, got the necessary help he needed, took the things he required and set out for the venue knowing he had a long way to travel. If he had left the chopped wood behind, he would not have been able to make the fire for the burnt offering. Adequate preparation prevents unpleasant surprises, aids adaptability and promotes success. In Abraham's case he did not know his faith and obedience to God was being tested. However, he did all the preparations beforehand that enabled him to pass the test. He probably passed the test of God as a result of his faithfulness to God, that is through his continual love and obedience to God. He had obeyed God in the past by leaving his father's house and journeying to a land God was going to show him without knowing where he was going yet obeying God's commands. Thus, he still obeyed in this instance.

Also, bear in mind that each result depends on the requirement of the test and unless these requirements are met one is bound to fail. God told him specifically to take his son Isaac, whom he loved so much and sacrifice him on one of the mountains at Moriah which he will point out to him. These were specific instructions that needed to be followed. He was to sacrifice Isaac and not his other son Ishmael. Also, he was to go to mount Moriah and no other mountain. God had already prepared a lamb waiting in the thicket for him to use instead of Isaac for the sacrifice and wanted him to specifically go there to sacrifice it. Should he have gone to a mountain other than he was told he would have ended up without the lamb. Of course, God is capable of providing a lamb everywhere as he is not limited in what he can do but I have come to the realisation that, his goodness is much appreciated through our love and obedience to him. If Abraham had done things his own way, he would have failed the test of obedience. Hence, why the need to follow God's instructions exactly. Adding to or taking away from the things God tells us and doing otherwise is disobedience to God and leads to failure to achieve what he has in store for us.

It is also necessary to stay focused without allowing distractions during a test hence, why examination rooms always have notices to ease distractions such as switching off mobile phones and staying silent until the end of the exam. Most people fail the test of life because of distractions from other people and things around them. Abraham told his servants at a point to stay and wait as he and Isaac went further for the sacrifice. If he had taken them further, then they might have realised that he was going to sacrifice Isaac. This would have made them say or do things to make him want to change his mind. Thus, preventing him from obeying God. Also, he did not allow Isaac's questioning of the whereabouts of the lamb to take his mind off what God had told him. When we are able to identify things that shift our focus from what we need to do to pass God's test, we will pass it.

We ought to remember that God does not allow his children to be tested above what they can bear. Neither does he allow temptation to come their way without a way of escape. If we desire to pass the test of God, we must endeavour to continually prepare ourselves by getting to know God (that is what he likes and dislikes through his word) and showing our love to him through our obedience to him.

Would you rather pass or fail the test of God?

CHAPTER QUESTIONS

&

THEMES FOR THOUGHT

- How did God test Abraham?
- What do you think would have happened if Abraham had failed his test of faith?
- Discuss 3 lessons you have learned from this chapter.

YOU CAN SUMMARISE YOUR THOUGHTS

YOU CAN REVISIT YOUR THOUGHTS

CHAPTER 23

GIVING A BEFITTING BURIAL

Then, leaving her body, he said to the Hittite elders, "Here I am, a stranger and a foreigner among you. Please sell me a piece of land so I can give my wife a proper burial." (NLT)

Genesis 23:3

MESSAGE AND LEARNING

Many of us would rather not read a chapter on death or burial but it is a fact of life that cannot be denied. Death is one of the most certain factors of life as there is no inherent trait within man to make him go on living in this earthly body forever. Death can happen slowly or suddenly to the young or the old, the rich or the poor, the strong or the weak and in a way, what is expected or unexpected. Yet, although these facts exist and statistics show there is one death every second in the world, the majority of us live without wanting to think, hear or talk about it, let alone prepare for it.

When a person dies, it will be undignified to treat the body with contempt. In that, the body is thrown away as to allow vultures or other such creatures to feast on it. In bible terms, a dignified way of parting company with the dead is to give a dignified burial. One that is befitting for the loved one who has passed on. Burying the dead is a way of saying a final goodbye to a person's life on earth. It is right therefore to give a befitting burial to a loved one when they pass on as that is the only final time, we could do anything for that loved one. Also, doing so gives us the opportunity to maintain their dignity even after death.

We read in this chapter that Sarah died at a ripe age at Hebron, a land in Canaan where she and Abraham sojourned. As they were strangers in the land, they had no land of their own to bury their dead. Abraham, not wanting to leave Sarah's corpse to the fate of the birds had to acquire a plot of land fit to be used as a burial place for his deceased wife. He first searched for a burial place he thought was appropriate to bury Sarah. Then, he inquired from the owner of the land if he could buy it. He did not accept land given to him by the Hittites even though they were willing to give it to him for free. He wanted to purchase the land out of a mark of respect for his wife's memory. Also, because the bible states he wanted a permanent burial place to use by his family in the foreign land. Abraham therefore searched for a plot of land that will meet this need, purchased it and buried Sarah there after mourning her.

We learn from this chapter that in terms of giving a befitting burial it is important to consider maintaining the dignity of the body even after the spirit has left it. Also, we don't just give anything because the person we have lost is not present to witness it. That is, we do the things we would have done for them had they still been alive. It would also be worthwhile taking into consideration the wish the person had before death and honouring it.

Having said all this, giving a befitting burial is important. However, it is equally important to treat the people around us with love, ensuring we maintain a good relationship with them in every possible way we could while they are still alive. Knowing that, we cannot do anything for them after death asides what we do for the body which has no life in it. Also, that, much as we might be able to maintain the dignity of a dead body and do all that is required for burial, it will be of much benefit and better appreciated by the person should they be shown love while they are still alive compared to putting more effort into giving a befitting burial to the body with no life. We are also better off showing kindness to a person when they are alive. By doing so, we will find it more rewarding and live with a clear conscience when we part company with them, knowing that we did the best we could for them in their lifetime.

Will you be willing to give a befitting burial to a loved one should you part company with them?

CHAPTER QUESTIONS

&

THEMES FOR THOUGHT

- Having learnt that each one of us is bound to die at a point in time of which none of us know when, what measures are you going to put in place in terms of your relationship with others?
- Why do you think it is morally wrong to just throw people away when they die?

YOU CAN SUMMARISE YOUR THOUGHTS

YOU CAN REVISIT YOUR THOUGHTS

CHAPTER 24

CHOOSING THE RIGHT PARTNER

Abraham was now very old, and the Lord had blessed him in every way. He said to the senior servant in his household, the one in charge of all that he had, "Put your hand under my thigh. I want you to swear by the Lord, the God of heaven and the God of earth, that you will not get a wife for my son from the daughters of the Canaanites, among whom I am living, but will go to my country and my own relatives and get a wife for my son Isaac." (NIV)

Genesis 24: 1-4

MESSAGE AND LEARNING

God intended marriage to be a lifelong relationship which ensured our holiness and happiness. Holiness in the sense that, we do all the things that will create a suitable relationship in which God would like to join in. Think about an environment of love, understanding, honesty and humility with God joined in a marriage, we are sure to enjoy the happiness for which he created. However, if marriage is intended to be lifelong then, it requires us to choose the right partner. Someone we will live with the whole of our lifetime. This makes choosing a potential partner to be married to a serious business. Any mistake made in choosing one in a casual way, could rob us of the happiness and all the good things made available to us by God.

We straight away read from the beginning of this chapter that, Abraham made his servant vow in the name of the Lord to choose the type of woman he wanted as a wife for his son. This shows how serious he took it and the fact that he wanted it done in the right way. He knew God's standards for marriage, accepted it and wanted his servant to vow to it. God was going to be a witness to him choosing the right partner for his son, Isaac. A wife of God's choice. Why then, is it that we at times ignore God's standard and choice for marriage and end up regretting our choices when we know perfectly well that God's choice is the best. God looks in the heart, at the intentions of that heart. But man looks at the outward appearance for example glamour, class and outward characteristics of a person, not really knowing what the person is really like. He sees the hidden intentions of the heart of man and knows a person more than anyone else does. Hence why, we should rely on his guidance and choice. He chose a woman who had beauty, an inward quality which increases for Isaac rather than glamour which is outward and fades away with time. Rebekah was beautiful, not just outwardly but also had the inner beauty of character. Also, she was God-fearing, submissive, polite, kind, caring and hardworking.

We realise in this chapter that certain key things were considered in choosing the right partner for Isaac. One of them was that Abraham consulted his oldest servant who helped in choosing a suitable wife for his son. He must have trusted his servant to put him in charge of all that he had in the first place. Also, his servant must have shown an extent of wisdom for him to have given him that responsibility. Additionally, being the oldest of his servants, it is likely that he would have turned many different corners in life than others and would have learnt from these experiences. Although, this might not always be true, there is always wisdom in the advice the elderly give. These reasons must have given Abraham the confidence to give his servant such responsibility of choosing the right partner for Isaac. Often, God who is all wise, chooses to pass on his wisdom through others to us. Especially through parents, grandparents and those who have turned many more corners than we have and who have learned the hard way in life. This teaches us the need to consult those who have already experienced marriage or know more about it and those who have spiritual authority over us, as the spirit of God leads us when choosing a marriage partner.

We also learn that Abraham asked him to choose a woman from the same background as he is. One of his own. It is important therefore, that we choose a partner of the same background, that is one who shares the same faiths and believes as we do. Reason being your faith determines your values: the things you cherish. When this happens, we have the same master controlling our lives. We submit together to the same ruler who we both would have to please. This makes it easier for us to reason together as we work towards the same goals. Thereby making it easier for us to achieve our goals in life. It also helps us in maintaining harmony in the decisions and choices we make and earns us the happiness we are expected to have. More so, it helps us get rid of disagreements and things that would rid us of the good things a good marriage has to offer.

It is also important to note, the first thing the servant did was to pray to God to lead him to God's choice of a partner for Isaac. Prayer cannot be taken out in our search for a life partner as doing so without prayer can lead us into a choice which is not a choice of God. We are therefore required to seek God's guidance through making choices. This is because, many may seem to be the right one in our search for a partner. Therefore, if we do not follow God's directions, we would fall into a trap of making the wrong choices. The servant knew young women from the village would be coming to draw water from the spring and any of them could be the right choice for Isaac. However, he needed God's help in deciding which one was meant for Isaac and that required him asking God through prayer.

Besides this, he considered qualities such as someone who was responsible, one who performed the duties required of her. The woman was to be one who came to draw water from the spring for her household chores. She also had to be kind in that she can share some of the water she had fetched through hard work with him. She had to be caring, in that she had to care not only for him but also for his camels. I wonder how many couples cared for not only their spouse but also the other people and things their spouse cared about: family, friends, colleagues and businesses. Rebekah was willing to draw water for the camels until they have had enough. She kept running quickly with the water to the camels to satisfy the need they had. Yet still, the servant did not rush into his conclusion that she was Isaac's future wife but rather waited for a confirmation.

How often have many come close to making a right choice, then they are deceived into making the wrong one instead because they lacked confirmation? Confirmation is important in that it settles a matter well and leads to the desired results. The servant waited for confirmation. He waited until he got to know she was the daughter of Bethuel. He praised God for it, remembering whatever we praise God for remains ours now and in the future.

We can see good qualities, not just in Rebekah but also her relatives which make us know God had led the servant into choosing the right wife for Isaac. For instance, Laban, Rebekah's brother run to the spring to welcome the servant, invited him home, offered the servant, the people he travelled with and the camels something to eat and cared for them. He also offered a listening ear to them. Rebekah's family also gave their blessings in the marriage which showed they were in support of them.

In all, Isaac accepted the wife of God's choice, Rebekah. Rebekah was a special comfort to Isaac in his hardest moments and Isaac loved Rebekah very much. This is what happens when we follow the right path in choosing a future partner. Would you rather choose your marriage partner the right way or otherwise?

CHAPTER QUESTIONS

&

THEMES FOR THOUGHT

- Why do you think it is necessary to seek God's guidance in choosing a marriage partner?
- So, the bible tells us Rebekah was beautiful. Can you list 3 characteristics which can make one beautiful?
- Why will you choose beauty over glamour?

YOU CAN SUMMARISE YOUR THOUGHTS

YOU CAN REVISIT YOUR THOUGHTS

CHAPTER 25

PRESENT SATISFACTION

"Once when Jacob was cooking some stew, Esau came in from the open country, famished. He said to Jacob, "Quick, let me have some of that red stew! I'm famished!" (That is why he was also called Edom). Jacob replied, "First sell me your birth right." "Look, I am about to die," Esau said. "What good is the birth right to me?" But Jacob said, "Swear to me first." So, he swore an oath to him, selling his birth right to Jacob. Then Jacob gave Esau some bread and some lentil stew. He ate and drank, and then got up and left. So, Esau despised his birth right." (NIV)

Genesis 25: 29-34

MESSAGE AND LEARNING

I want it now is the song of the day. People want everything now or never. We simply do not want to wait a little longer when we can satisfy our desires with things other than the real ones. We all are faced at certain times of our lives with situations in which we are tempted to satisfy the fleeting desires we have had instantly, ignoring the consequences that come with our actions.

Think of a child who has a test at hand to revise for and knows not doing so could result in failure and other associated bad consequences. Yet, being unable to forfeit the desire to play games or watch television goes ahead to play or watch and should they fail the test, later regret the consequences of their decisions and actions. We can also think of an example in which rather than waiting to enter marriage before sleeping with the people we intend to marry; youngsters satisfy their sexual desire by having premarital sex and having broken their virginity or ended up with a venereal disease or in the wrong relationship later regret the consequences of their actions. Some, later find out if they had waited a little longer, would have met the right partner or made a better choice.

Sometimes, not making a conscious effort to weigh up the options and the related consequences, can lead us into satisfying desires we have now and regretting our actions later. Other times, our unwillingness to delay our instant pressing desires until we can find what gives lasting satisfaction causes us to miss out on the best life has to offer. Also, placing our desires over the perfect plan of God, leaves us with regret.

In this chapter we find out that Esau returns home hungry from hunting. He had an instant desire to satisfy his hunger. We are also told of the fact that he met his brother Jacob preparing soup and he asked for some of it. Jacob, crafty as he was, requires his brother to bind himself to the sale of his birth right before giving him some of the stew. Still, the birth right was more valuable and important than the plate of stew. Being the firstborn son, Esau was entitled to a birth right. Having the birth right meant he could have a double portion of all the money and property his father Isaac owned and would become the head of the family when he died (Deuteronomy 21:17). This meant he would have more wealth, authority and respect than his brother Jacob and any other siblings he was to have. He was therefore expected to cherish his birth right, treat it with great value rather than treat it lightly. The desire he had at the time of satisfying his hunger however, led him to trade his birth right which was of great and lasting value. He seemed not to have valued it. Neither did he take care to protect it. For in fact, if we cherish what we have or has been given to us, we will do all we can to protect it. We would choose what is of value over what is not. But here is the case in which Esau treated what he had with contempt. He would rather have a plate of instant stew than a blessing when his father died, and he traded his blessing for it.

We live in a world in which the things we see and hear around us, our culture and laws passed by the government cause us to satisfy our desires instantly. When in-fact, these desires are far away from the things that will benefit us and the will of God, we still go ahead and do them anyway. We are deceived into following our heart desires in the moment without thinking of what it would cost us should we do so. We desire to have sex when we want to, in the wrong way, with whoever we want, if they consent to it. Thereby putting our feelings above what God has planned for us, to enjoy in marriage in the right way. We are basically encouraged into being like Esau. But, in the letter to the Hebrews, we are told not to be like Esau who regretted his bargain and afterwards sought his father's blessings with tears but there was no repentance nor recovery of what given up. He was indifferent about the fact that he had exchanged his birth right. His fleeting instant desire led him to despise the eternal plan of God for his life. He had traded the best for the worst and was not going to ever get it back again. If we choose to satisfy the fleeting desires of our flesh with things other than wait for what God has planned for us, we will not inherit the good things God has in store for us, just as Esau never inherited the blessings of his birth right.

Would you rather deny yourself of the present satisfaction of the flesh and inherit all the blessings God has in store for you?

CHAPTER QUESTIONS

&

THEMES FOR THOUGHT

- What are your thoughts on pre-marital sex? Good or bad? Why?
- What should Esau have done differently from exchanging his birth right for food?

YOU CAN SUMMARISE YOUR THOUGHTS

YOU CAN REVISIT YOUR THOUGHTS

CHAPTER 26

PROSPERING IN THE MIDST OF ADVERSITIES

"Abandoning that one, Isaac moved on and dug another well. This time there was no dispute over it, so Isaac named the place Rehoboth (which means "open space"), for he said, "At last the LORD has created enough space for us to prosper in this land." (NLT)

Genesis 26: 22

MESSAGE AND LEARNING

No matter what we choose to do in life, there will be resistance. The resistance we face depends on the worth of the reward of the actions we take or would like to take. If you want to get top grades in school, you will have to invest in an equal amount of time and effort that can earn you the grades you expect. But this also comes with the denial of certain pleasures you might want to enjoy which in fact can prevent or stop you from getting your aim or goal. Newton, one of the greatest scientists the world has ever had, stated in his third law, that for every action, there is an equal and opposite reaction. The size of the force of an action is equal in magnitude to the size of the opposing force. Which indicates that an action greater than the opposing force is needed should that action yield the required results. Much the same, in our pursuit to achieve our goals and desires in life, we should be prepared to face challenges equivalent to what we expect to achieve. Also, gain an understanding of the fact that these challenges might try to stop us or make us want to withdraw into our old state and should what we want to achieve be important to us, be prepared to act in a way to overcome these challenges.

Can you think of the many times you have wanted to break away from an old way that was ruining your life with difficulty and probably could not do so? Are there times that you have embarked on a journey in life but later turned back midway because of stumbling blocks that were in your way? Have you ever desired to pursue a career knowing very well that it could pave way for you in the future to get your dream job, and bring you great benefits and the satisfaction you have always wanted? But challenges life threw at you made you quit? The truth is nothing good comes to us in an easy way. We have to strive to get the good things in life. The only time we can reach our expected ends in life is when we have been able to go through the situation that befalls us without quitting, face the challenges squarely and overcome them. Unless we make up our mind and take the necessary steps needed to achieve our dreams and the purpose of God in our lives, we will continue to live short of God's expectations for us and probably never achieve our aims and goals in life.

This chapter presents with Isaac in the land of Gerar at a time when there was famine and drought. It was a land in which he was to prosper. A place which God had promised to give to him and his descendants and bless all the nations of the world through them. Yet, it was not a place free of challenges. Mind you, God never promised him that he would not face any challenges but rather he promised him of his constant presence with him and this also meant being with him through the challenging times. We read in this chapter that he went ahead to sow in the land even though there was drought. Yet, he harvested tremendous crops. He reaped a hundred times more grain than he planted although conditions at the time did not favour a good yield. This made him prosper in unending wealth acquiring large flocks of sheep and goats, great herds of cattle and he had many servants who assisted him throughout his journey. This must have come with obedience to God, hard work and being hopeful of only achieving the best.

Asides the challenges of living on a land where there was famine and drought, he also had fears of losing his life and also his wife to another man. This would have destabilised his state of security in the land as well, however, he continued to live there.

Apart from this, Isaac had to put up with not just pressures that came from nature (such as the harsh weather) but also hostile attitudes of the people that surrounded him. Just as he managed to solve the issue of drought by attaining wells that supplied water for both his flock and crops and began to see an increase in his yield. The Philistines noticed he was prospering, and they filled up all the wells he had with earth through envy. To add to this, Abimelech, king of the Philistines ordered him to move from his location of prosperity. He moved to the Gerar valley, "a lowly state," to start all over again. There, he reopened the wells that were previously filled up and his shepherds also dug new ones but soon these were claimed by the local shepherds. Notice that this also did not stop him from his pursuit of finding a spring through digging a well. However, the local people fought him over his next one and he lost it to them. Eventually, the local people left him alone after digging a new well: He finally had the space to himself and there was enough room for him to prosper. If he had given up along the way, he certainly would not have achieved the wealth he had gained.

However, through determination, persistence, perseverance, hard work and being resilient without giving in to the challenging situations he faced, he was able to prosper in the midst of adversity. It also required having hope for the future, and confidence in himself and also in God's promises. He could have chosen to allow the challenges he faced to stop him receiving God's blessings, but he did not.

Would you rather persevere through challenges in life or give up at the face of adversity?

CHAPTER QUESTIONS

&

THEMES FOR THOUGHT

- Write two things you will do during challenging situations to help you prosper?
- What one thing have you observed from your family background that could be against you prospering in life?
- What can you do in order to prosper in life?

YOU CAN SUMMARISE YOUR THOUGHTS

YOU CAN REVISIT YOUR THOUGHTS

CHAPTER 27

HARD WORK

Isaac: "Yours will be no life of ease and luxury, but you shall hew your way with your sword. For a time, you will serve your brother, but you will finally shake loose from him and be free." (TLB)

Genesis 27: 39-40

MESSAGE AND LEARNING

Having the right start in life makes it easier to have a successful future life. However, as we do not get to choose our backgrounds this is not always the case. Some of us may feel disadvantaged having come from a broken home or being poor or not having such a well to do family or would have been brought up by parents who had a minimal education, which can contribute to us having a difficult start in life. However, although the listed circumstances and more may contribute to us not having the right start in life, and hinder our success, they do not ultimately determine our future success. We can have some disadvantages from our background and still succeed in life. The truth is, we can choose how we allow these disadvantages to affect our lives. It is our response to the situations we find ourselves in, that determine what we are or become and not necessarily the situations themselves. One way by which we can overcome the challenges we face and succeed in life is by seeking God's help and direction and be willing to follow his guidance. Also, apart from the fact that God is with us as believers and helps us in our endeavours, when we work hard, we can evolve our future lives.

Hard work they say never kills anybody. Rather it plays a key role in ensuring we fulfil our purpose on earth and get to where we expect to be in life.

Of course, God's original plan for man was not to engage him in hard work. His will for man was not to labour to earn a living. God did all the hard work through creation and created man to look after what he had created and to rule over it.

He made work to be good for us, one that was suitable, enjoyable and not exhausting. It was God's delight seeing man enjoy this duty assigned to him while doing it faithfully. However, through disobedience and the fall of man, work became exhausting. Subsequently, man had to toil in working the ground in order to earn a living from it. He was also going to battle with the thorns and thistles which grew from the ground making work even more exhausting. With difficulty man had to work until he returned to the ground. Depending on the choices made by our predecessors and the choices we make; work could even be harder.

Yet, it is morally wrong for one to make their work the biggest thing in life and to live for it in the search for success in life. As by doing so, it becomes one's idol and this is wrong. Much the same, it is morally wrong to be lazy and not work. This is because, you not only deny others the service you were made to offer them and hence waste whatever gift God has given you (which is wrong) but also, you end up struggling even more to provide for yourself, those who depend on you and also the poor and needy. Knowing where to place work in one's life, not making it one's idol but then working as hard as we ought to, is part of everybody's duty.

We read in this chapter that Jacob tricked his blind aged father to get the blessings he was going to give Esau before he died. Esau returned from his hunting trip and prepared his father's favourite dish, only to realise his brother had already received all the blessings and there were none left for him. Getting the blessings would have made life easier for Esau. He would have been the master of his brothers and had many nations serve him. He would also have had the best of land with plenty of dew for healthy crops and a good harvest of grain and wine. But here is the case in which he did not have what would have given him that easy start to make it in life. The only other option he had left was to work hard if he wanted to succeed. He was to live off the land and what it yields, live by the sword (serve his brother for a time until he became successful). We however get to know from subsequent chapters (chapters 33, 34) that by working hard he was more or less as successful as his brother Jacob.

We work hard at a task when we put in our best both mentally and physically to get the best results. This comes with having a mental attitude of getting things done in the right way and also persevering through challenging times and situations to achieve *perceived* results. In the same way, we would be required to put in consistent physical effort in whatever we do. This can be achieved by cutting down on leisure time, not cutting corners, avoiding distractions while working and spending adequate and quality time with our work. It also requires setting our priorities right and doing things faithfully. By doing all these in the right way, we too can succeed in life even if things are not easy from the start.

Do you choose to work hard from now onwards?

CHAPTER QUESTIONS

&

THEMES FOR THOUGHT

- State and explain 3 qualities we can find in hard working people.
- What would have happened to Esau if he had decided to be slothful?

YOU CAN SUMMARISE YOUR THOUGHTS

YOU CAN REVISIT YOUR THOUGHTS

CHAPTER 28

OBEDIENCE TO PARENTS

"Now Esau learned that Isaac had blessed Jacob and had sent him to Paddan Aram to take a wife from there, and that when he blessed him he commanded him, "Do not marry a Canaanite woman," and that Jacob had obeyed his father and mother and had gone to Paddan Aram." (NIV)

Genesis 28: 6&7

MESSAGE AND LEARNING

Obedience to our parents is the first of God's commandments with a promise. In obeying our parents, we submit to their authority and do as we are told. By obeying our parents, we indirectly obey God also, as he has instructed us to do so. The opposite being true, in that when we choose to disobey our parents, we disobey God. Coming to this realisation makes it easier for us to obey our parents as we understand God says so and wants us to do so. It is doing what we are told that makes us obedient, first to God, then to our parents. When we obey our parents, the bible tells us it may go well with us and that we may enjoy a long life on earth.

Most people however find it difficult obeying this simple command of God with a belief that it is impossible to obey a parent who acts in a wrong way. But then, it is right to obey our parents. Although our parents can sometimes get things wrong, we have a choice and responsibility to obey them whilst, not following in their footsteps. This is because although God will hold them responsible for their wrong actions and negative influences on our lives, God will hold us accountable if we follow suit in the same or similar wrong ways.

I have engaged in conversations with younger adults who explain they find their parents doing the wrong things most of the time and this makes it difficult for them to obey them when these parents tell them to do the right things. But the truth is, we must obey our parents, and do as we are told, if what we are told is the right thing to do even if our parents do not do the right things themselves. This is because our parents are humans, and they too can make mistakes and as already stated God will hold them responsible for their own actions. We are therefore to do the right things we are told to do without allowing the bad acts to influence us. I call this 'looking the other way'. That is, although I see someone do the wrong thing, I decide to do the right thing rather than copy the bad act. The reason being, our eye is a channel through which Satan can deceive us to sin. We see this in the book of Genesis when he caused man to disobey God by eating off the tree of knowledge of good and evil when they knew they should not eat off it, as God had warned them not to. Also, David's eye caused him to sin, and he disobeyed God when he committed adultery and the sins that followed it. He knew he should not have slept with Uriah's wife but went ahead and did it as a result of what he saw. Although in the two examples, man and David both fell to the temptation of the eye and disobeyed God, we find out that, Jesus obeyed God when Satan showed him all the kingdoms of the world and the glory of them. He did not allow his eyes to cause him to sin. Therefore, Jesus tells us in the book of Matthew that, if the eyes cause us to sin it is better, we get rid of it. Simply put, 'look the other way', ignore its influence on you and do not give any attention to it. In the same way, we should not allow the bad influences of our parents to impact our lives, but we must obey them.

It is also understandable that some may find it difficult doing as they are told in situations when a parent is to advise one in doing the wrong thing. However, if one is to respectfully explain their reasons why such an act is not the right thing to do, they would have equally obeyed the parent. Aside this, if we humble ourselves and learn lessons from the bad experiences and the consequences of the bad acts from our parents, we will gain wisdom, which will help us avoid similar choices, experiences and consequences.

As already mentioned, we must obey our parents as God says and we will receive his promise as an added benefit. Also, it is right for us to obey our parents as they have been around many different corners than we have and have gained experience which we could benefit from, if we need it. Asides this, I believe no parent will wish their child evil, and although some of the things they may want us to do may be wrong, I believe they tell us with good intentions. Hence why, we should humbly and respectfully explain our reasons why we believe those things are wrong and should not be done.

In this chapter, we learn of how Isaac said to his son Jacob not to marry a Canaanite woman but go to Paddan-Aram and marry from the house of Bethuel. The instructions were *not to* marry a Canaanite woman but *to* marry from the house of Bethuel. We also, read in this chapter that Isaac not only sent his son off but that he attached blessings to the instructions he gave him. The only way Jacob was to receive the attached blessings, however, was to first obey the instructions he was given. If he just offered a listening ear and did not do as he was told, he would not have received any of the added blessings. We also, learn in this chapter that people watch our acts of obedience, and this influences the decisions they make regarding similar choices that befall them. Take note of the following four points.

Firstly, Jacob's obedience to his father motivated his brother Esau to do likewise. In that, by obeying his father, Jacob set an example to his brother Esau to follow in. Thus, Esau in addition to the wives he already had, married Mahalath who was not a Canaanite woman. This also tells us there was something peculiar about Jacob's obedience that had made Esau want to do the same. I believe one of them is the fact that, they each enjoyed blessings from their parents whenever they obeyed them. Esau knew things will go well with his brother if he did as he was told to do, hence followed in his obedience. Secondly, we read that Jacob was also able to meet God at a place he later named Bethel. This teaches us that when we obey our parents, God is happy, and he stays with us through our obedience. It is actually in our obedience to God that we enjoy his company, comfort and constant supply. Thirdly, all the blessings Jacob's father pronounced on him were confirmed by God through the dream he had, and they surely came to pass. Why, because God honours his promise and for the fact that he has attached a promise to obedience to our parents, he had to ensure he did so. God was with him and protected him, God made his descendants numerous and through them blessed all the nations of the earth. What's more, he got to marry a wife who was not just glamorous but beautiful, a woman he loved.

Do you choose to disobey your parents and miss out on their blessings and God's blessings? Or will you rather obey them and receive their blessings and all that God promises?

CHAPTER QUESTIONS

&

THEMES FOR THOUGHT

- Give two ways in which it may go well with you if you honour your parents.
- Give one example in which a parent can be in the wrong, but a child can still honour the parent.
- Can you give an example of a situation in which if a person is to honour their parents, they will avoid death and enjoy long life on the earth as the bible says in Ephesians 6:2-3?

YOU CAN SUMMARISE YOUR THOUGHTS

YOU CAN REVISIT YOUR THOUGHTS

CHAPTER 29

DECEPTION

"Jacob was in love with Rachel and said, "I'll work for you seven years in return for your younger daughter Rachel." (NIV)

Genesis 29:18

"And in the morning, behold, it was Leah! And Jacob said to Laban, "What is this you have done to me? Did I not serve with you for Rachel? Why then have you deceived me?"

Genesis 29:25

MESSAGE AND LEARNING

Deception is an act of making someone believe something that is not true. A person is therefore deceived when they are presented with what is not actually the real thing. For example, Information can be communicated in a way to mislead others. This can happen when important parts of the information communicated are omitted, extra or irrelevant information is added, or vital parts are changed making it difficult for the person being deceived to get a true understanding of what is being said. When this happens the one being deceived ends up making the wrong decisions and taking misguided actions. Also, the appearance of things or people can be changed and presented to us in a way to deceive us. If we are not careful, we will be deceived into believing what has been presented to us is the true thing.

Sometimes, people we are in a relationship with, be it friendly, marital or business relations, might want to deceive us in some way. We realise that most deception is as a result of the deceiver seeking personal gain or taking advantage of the one being deceived. While some may want to deceive you to make a decision that will end you up in trouble or disgrace, others may want to deceive you, so you lose something important or just to cause your downfall in life. It could be done out of jealousy, hatred, envy or sheer ignorance.

Here in this chapter, we find Laban deceived Jacob on several occasions. In one these instances, he knew perfectly well he was not going to give Rachel to Jacob for marriage (as per their custom, Leah who was the oldest should be given in marriage first). Yet, he deceived Jacob into believing he was going to give him Rachel, made him work for seven years they both agreed on but instead he was deceived and given Leah. To make matters worse, he did not inform Jacob when the time of the marriage was due of his intent of giving him Leah as his wife, instead of Rachel. This could have probably prevented Jacob going to bed with Leah. Rather, Leah was veiled all through the wedding and they went to bed in the dark only for Jacob to find out on the morning of his honeymoon that he had Leah and not Rachel.

Three distinct features that allowed for the deception to take place can be identified in this instance.

Firstly, we find out darkness (hidden agenda) was at play. As already mentioned, Leah was veiled throughout the wedding and went to bed in the dark with Jacob. Her appearance was therefore hidden by the veil and the darkness of the night made it impossible for her to be noticed. This teaches us to watch out for situations in which things presented to us are concealed in a manner unexpected to us or information presented to us is unclear hence not easily understood. Are you given things by people who would not want anyone else to know about it and you seem not to understand the reason behind it? Do people want to go into an important agreement with you and will only do that on condition that key people who can guide you in the right direction stay out of it? Do you sometimes question or have an intuition of something not seeming right in an act portrayed by someone leading you into doing something? Just pause, and ensure you make meaning out of the dark cues surrounding a circumstance before you decide on the next steps to prevent being deceived.

Secondly, overindulgence could have played a part and made it possible for deception to take place. It is very likely Jacob had more wine at the feast in celebration of the marriage than he should have had and would have been drunk to an extent of not detecting it was Leah and not Rachel. For he had lived with them long enough to recognise their voices, figure and certain distinct features about each of them which could have guided his actions of ending up in bed with Leah even if she was veiled and there was darkness. Situations which can alter our emotions such as enjoyment of what we long for can result in overindulgence and cause us to be irrational in our decision making. Studies have shown that our emotions at particular times play a key role in the decision-making process. We are less likely to consider risks associated with the decisions we make and rather underestimate them in situations where we have more than we need, are given the things we longed for, are in a state of excitement or celebration. All these things can lead to us making unrealistic decisions in the moment. It is therefore vital that we do not make hasty decisions during times when our emotions are running high, so we avoid being misled or deceived. Although some may have genuine intentions behind their actions towards us, it is important that we are careful not to be lured into making decisions because people lavish us with gifts or treat us in exceptionally kind ways in return for other gestures from us.

Thirdly, information was communicated in a misleading manner as to lead to deception. Laban knew very well that their custom did not allow the marrying off, of the youngest daughter ahead of the first born and should have relayed this important information to Jacob before the agreement was made. But this was hidden from Jacob. When we receive information therefore, which lacks vital details which can help us in planning; it is necessary that we ensure we ask the relevant questions which can lead us to get sufficient information before deciding on the outcome. Also, in situations where too much information is given to us which overwhelms us and we are unable to make out salient aspects of what is being communicated, it is important we seek clarity before coming to a final decision. Simply put, when unsure about something, ask the right questions until you have all the information you need to guide you in your decision making.

It is important that we learn from this chapter to be careful not to be deceived by others. This could help guide the decision-making process and avoid making mistakes and living with regrets. Will you be careful and watch out for the right cues in order not to be deceived?

CHAPTER QUESTIONS

&

THEMES FOR THOUGHT

- What are your thoughts on why people deceive others?
- In what way could you be deceived by someone else?

YOU CAN SUMMARISE YOUR THOUGHTS

YOU CAN REVISIT YOUR THOUGHTS

CHAPTER 30

ENVY OR JEALOUSY

"When Rachel saw that she was not bearing Jacob any children, she became ***jealous*** *of her sister. So, she said to Jacob, "Give me children, or I'll die!" (NIV)*

Genesis 30:1

Now when Rachel saw that she bore Jacob no children, Rachel ***envied*** *her sister, and said to Jacob, "Give me children, or else I die!" (KJV)*

Genesis 30:1

MESSAGE AND LEARNING

This chapter begins straight away with Rachel expressing her feelings as a result of the state she was in, to her husband Jacob. She was envious of Leah because she saw Leah in a situation which placed her in a more advantageous position than she was. She wanted something that she was lacking but her rival Leah had, that is children. This made her envy Leah. But, considering she was more loved by Jacob than Leah was, lived in the fear of losing the love and affection received from Jacob, if she does not bear children to him. This made her jealous. Although desiring what someone else has is envy and being fearful of losing what you have is jealousy, these two words are normally used interchangeably.

Here is the situation in which Rachel's envy and jealousy of Leah caused her to experience deep sadness to an extent of her wanting to die. In most cases envy or jealousy causes people to dislike others, act in an angry way towards them and makes it difficult for them to share in their success or joy. The envy and jealousy she experienced made her act in a way that made Jacob angry. Also, it made her hasty and make unwise decisions, in that she gave her servant Bilhah to Jacob to sleep with to give her children without realising God was going to give her children of her own. It also resulted in an unhealthy competition between both her and Leah as each gave their servant to Jacob so they could have children through them.

We get to find out that people who get envious of others lack the knowledge of diversity in nature. They probably might never have known or come to the realisation that we are all different in our own ways. Although humans were created in the image of God, no two persons are the same. We were each created to accomplish particular purposes in life and for this reason have been given suitable abilities required to achieve these purposes.

Even though both Rachel and Leah were married to Jacob, they lived separate lives and God had different plans for them. If Rachel had consoled herself with the knowledge of being different from Leah and having a purpose in life different to hers, she probably would have done things differently.

When we stop comparing ourselves to others knowing that everyone has their strengths and weaknesses in life, and that no two people were ever created the same, then we will not envy others. Also, by trusting God in the sense that, he is able to turn all situations around no matter how difficult we see them and give freely to all, thus gives one a sense of hope in life and enables one to boldly approach God in prayer with their requests. We later find out in this chapter that, in God's own time, he remembered Rachel and gave her children, after she sought God in prayer. Also, one of her children (Joseph) became the saviour to his family and the entire nation of Egypt at a time of the famine.

Why choose to be jealous or envious of others when you could ask God in prayer for the things you need?

CHAPTER QUESTIONS

&

THEMES FOR THOUGHT

- Why do you think we should not envy or be jealous of others?
- What should we do instead in situations where we feel the need for the things we lack?

YOU CAN SUMMARISE YOUR THOUGHTS

YOU CAN REVISIT YOUR THOUGHTS

CHAPTER 31

TOLERANCE

"So, Jacob sent word to Rachel and Leah to come out to the fields where his flocks were. He said to them, "I see that your father's attitude toward me is not what it was before, but the God of my father has been with me. You know that I've worked for your father with all my strength, yet your father has cheated me by changing my wages ten times. However, God has not allowed him to harm me."

Genesis 31:4-7

MESSAGE AND LEARNING

Each one of us has our own values and beliefs in life. Depending on them, together with our attitudes, we tend to get on well with the people who think and behave in similar ways to us. When we share the same likes and dislikes, love to do the same things or go to the same places and share a common opinion with others, it is much easier getting on well with them. Likewise, the opposite is true. We find it difficult being around people whose behaviours differ from our own and our reluctance to accept these differences is known as intolerance. We can especially get intolerant to people who continually do things we disagree with or dislike; things that do not make us happy. However, the ability to continually forebear with practices which differ from one's own is known as tolerance.

Prior to going to live with his uncle Laban, Jacob had his own dreams and aspirations. He felt a need to get married to one of his uncle Laban's daughters and not to a Canaanite woman. His father Isaac had pronounced the blessings of having many children and having a great assembly of nations through his descendants on him. On his way to Paddan-aran, where his uncle lived, he had an encounter with the Lord God who confirmed his father's blessings and assured him he was going to be with him and bless him in many other ways. This must have given him an expectation of having his need of a wife met and his dream of becoming wealthy, come to pass as he journeyed on to Paddan-aran.

However, not long after living with his uncle he found out that he disliked most of his uncle's actions towards him. Firstly, he offered him work for a longer amount of time in return for the right to marry his daughter. Also, Laban changed his attitude towards Jacob as he was not treating him with the same kindness he was used to. More so, he cheated him by changing his wages ten times. Yet, Jacob was able to tolerate his uncle's behaviour for the next twenty years whilst he lived with him. He was faced with the choice of whether to tolerate these actions until his needs and aspirations were met. Jacob chose to be tolerant to his uncle's cruel behaviour and stayed on until the angel of the Lord told him to leave. By being tolerant until God's appointed time, Jacob had his needs met and achieved his aspirations. He got to marry Rachel in the end and was blessed with flocks, herds, camels, servants, wives and children.

Most of the time, we find ourselves in similar situations. For example, one might be in a career in which they are seeking progression and find that a superior who should be assisting them in this way is treating them in a way as to make them want to give up. They might feel they are being discriminated against, not supported, underpaid or not liked. But by focussing on their dream and tolerating the behaviours around them they could eventually achieve their goals at the set time. Similarly, a child might at some point feel they are being picked on and treated badly by their teacher for some reason and want to stop schooling. However, through tolerance and a decision to stay on, it will benefit them in the end. Their performance could be improved, and they could get their dream career.

Jacob's tolerance with his uncle Laban teaches us that although it can be difficult tolerating others, when we are able to, God can use the situation to work for our good. Also, we can get our needs met and achieve our dreams and aspirations. The benefits we derive should motivate us to be tolerant until the set time to part company or move on in life. More so, we learn not to be too hasty in leaving situations without a word from God, particularly when following the directions of God and we find ourselves surrounded by circumstances that make us want to give up.

Do you find yourself living with someone or in a career or an institution where someone is doing something you dislike? Are you willing to be tolerant until the set time or not? What choice do you make?

CHAPTER QUESTIONS

&

THEMES FOR THOUGHT

- How would you explain the term tolerance?
- How would you tolerate a sibling or a teacher who treats you in a way you dislike?
- What do you think are some of the advantages of tolerating others?

YOU CAN SUMMARISE YOUR THOUGHTS

YOU CAN REVISIT YOUR THOUGHTS

CHAPTER 32

RECONCILIATION

"Jacob sent messengers ahead of him to his brother Esau in the land of Seir, the country of Edom. He instructed them: "This is what you are to say to my lord Esau: 'Your servant Jacob says, I have been staying with Laban and have remained there till now. I have cattle and donkeys, sheep and goats, male and female servants. Now I am sending this message to my lord, that I may find favour in your eyes."

Genesis 32:3-5

MESSAGE AND LEARNING

There might be times in our lives, when the things we said or did would have knowingly or not, offended the people around us. When this happens, the good relationship once enjoyed is strained and, in some instances, results in a breakdown in relationships. Communication that existed is no longer the way it used to be, attitudes towards each other change, leading to temporary or permanent separation. But when this happens, the purpose for which the persons or parties involved (be it married partners, family, friends or colleagues) were brought together is not achieved. It could also lead to one or both parties living with a sense of guilt, hatred or frustration for the time the separation exists. More so, prayers might be hindered, and blessings delayed as a result of this. However, reconciliation gives a sense of relief and restores peace and serenity within a person. It allows one to receive God's forgiveness and acceptance making way for God's blessings.

It is important that we seek reconciliation once we realise someone has something against us and it has resulted in a breakdown in the relationship. The reason being we might at the initial stage fail to accept responsibility for a breakdown in the relationship, but if it turns out to be that we were in the wrong, we will end up paying a lot more for the consequences than if we had accepted responsibility at the initial stage. We would rather suffer less shame, guilt and feelings of withdrawal from the other person if we seek reconciliation in the first instance.

It is for our benefit to do so as it saves us from lots of regrets in the future if we realise we were in the wrong in the first place. Particularly when we do something against someone, we are indebted to them and will only be freed of it after we have settled matters. However, if we were in the right, it gives us more fulfilment having realised we have saved a relationship and the benefits of it. Hence, why Jesus advises us, to leave our gifts at the altar and first go and be reconciled to whoever has something against us before coming to offer our gifts. Doing so gives us relief from guilt, improves our mental and physical well-being and above all restores our relationship with God.

Reconciliation according to the Oxford dictionary is an act of restoring friendly relations. Through my study of the Scriptures, I have come to terms with key considerations that should be made if a broken relationship is to be restored in the right way.

Firstly, it is important that whoever seeks to reconcile with another person sees the need to do so and is ready to accept responsibility for what went wrong, although this might not always be their fault. If the existing conflict or separation has been caused by them, they make it their aim not to repeat it again. Although it will be good to feel remorseful for a wrong act, scripture has proven being in a state of repentance is the best, as it is very likely a remorseful person will do whatever they did again. Doing so places them in a good stance of achieving their goal of receiving forgiveness and having the relationship restored. However, depending on who is involved and what caused the breakdown of a friendly relationship, reconciliation might be challenging in that, it is not everyone who will willingly want to be reconciled after a breakdown in a relationship. Whereas some may gladly accept an apology and allow a broken relationship to be easily reconciled, others might for different reasons hinder it. We should however not be discouraged when we see the need to be reconciled unto others and are being challenged in ways not to do so, knowing the benefits it gives. The bible encourages us to go the extra mile in order to seek reconciliation until we have done all that is expected of us.

There is a need to also pray for God's lead and wisdom in how to go about the act of reconciliation considering the challenges involved. Also, as each situation will be different from the other and because we as humans react in different ways to different situations, God's guidance is needed hence why we must pray. In some cases, the other party could be bitter about the whole situation that brought about the breakdown in the relationship in the first place, unwilling to be reconciled or even wanting to pay back what has been done to them to the extent that the role played by God will be crucial to restoring the relationship. Hence why, prayer should not be taken out of this act. Prayer calms storms. Prayer can turn difficult situations into positive outcomes. It also grants favour in that we are accepted in situations in which we could be rejected. Remember, the king's heart is in the hands of the Lord, as the rivers of water, he turns it wherever he wills. God can cause situations to change with prayer to allow for our acceptance in situations where we could have been rejected.

Another key aspect of the reconciliation process is humility. There is a need for the person seeking reconciliation to humble themselves in every way to make it possible. It will be improper for the person seeking reconciliation to be judgemental about the other person, attempt to defend themselves or try to give reasons why they acted in the way they did. Doing any of these will only stir up more anger, resentment, bitterness and hurt, and make matters worse. There is an Egyptian proverb which states that "The boat that has two captains, sinks". Or in other words two masters cannot steer a boat to safe landing. In the same way a boat with two captains, neither of whom wants to be subordinate and listen to the other, will easily get lost at sea. So will two parties seeking reconciliation, with neither wanting to humble themselves, get anywhere near restoring the peace and friendly relationship that once existed. Rather it may make matters worse.

In some situations, it will be a good idea to appease the other person by giving him or her something as an act of restitution. Doing so causes the other party to see how much effort is being put into restoring the once broken relationship and goes a long way to pacify the soul of the person who has been offended. A man's gift makes room for him.

For the twenty years Jacob was away from home, he might have been living with a sense of guilt of how he treated his brother Esau prior to their separation. Twice he had deceived Esau. Firstly, by taking his birth right and then stealing his blessings. Esau hated him for this and planned to kill him. However, in his desperation to kill his brother, he found out Jacob had left for Paddan-Aram. The friendly relationship between them had been destroyed by his deceptive acts. However, he saw the need to be reconciled with his brother when he had to return to his place of birth. Just as has already been stated in earlier paragraphs, Jacob accepted responsibility for the breakdown in the relationship and was ready to seek reconciliation. He did this by first preparing himself and his family to be reconciled with Esau. He also prayed committing the situation into God's hands. For he needed God's favour and guidance in the whole situation as he knew his brother would have killed him if he was to meet him. He was so fearful of his brother and had no idea of what he had planned to do to him if he were to meet him. So, he prayed. In his desperation of wrestling with the angel of God for blessings, he sought for the favour of God in that his brother would look favourably upon him and not harm him upon his return. He sought God's deliverance in prayer in that his life will be preserved. Also, so his brother would listen to him and accept his plea. Jacob sent humbling messages to his brother prior to meeting him and humbled himself before Esau when they met. As well as that, he presented gifts to his brother prior to going before him. Thus, by undertaking all these things the brothers were reconciled.

In all, if we carefully choose our words and act in a loving way, relationships will grow stronger and not be strained nor broken. Hence, there will be no need for a reconciliation.

CHAPTER QUESTIONS

&

THEMES FOR THOUGHT

- What steps can you personally follow to reconcile with someone who has something against you?
- List and explain 3 qualities that can be found in people who seek reconciliation.
- What are the benefits of reconciliation?

YOU CAN SUMMARISE YOUR THOUGHTS

YOU CAN REVISIT YOUR THOUGHTS

CHAPTER 33

RUNNING AT YOUR OWN PACE

But Jacob replied, "You can see, my lord, that some of the children are very young, and the flocks and herds have their young, too. If they are driven too hard, even for one day, all the animals could die. Please, my lord, go ahead of your servant. We will follow slowly, at a pace that is comfortable for the livestock and the children. I will meet you at Seir." (NLT)

Genesis 33:13&14

MESSAGE AND LEARNING

The only people who win a race with success are those who keep their eyes on the track assigned to them without giving in to distractions that may come their way. By staying focused, one is able to direct all the available resources they have into winning the race. The time and effort given to distractions can all be channelled into getting our aims met when we stay focused and keep to our pace.

However, as other people may also be running alongside us either in the same or a different race of life it is important that we learn to run at our own pace. We could get discouraged, feel exhausted or frustrated by focussing on the pace at which other people are running their own races of life, be unable to give our best and even give up if we do not keep to our own pace.

People who keep to other people's pace, give more of their attention to what others are doing rather than concentrating on what they are meant to do. They tend to copy what others are doing and are prospering in and fail to see the advantages they have compared to these people. More specifically they always want to match up with others whilst neglecting their potentials in life. For instance, it is not a must for one to jump into marriage because they see their contemporaries getting married, particularly if they have not found the right partner. Much the same, it will be unwise to follow in an act of someone else or run at their pace when in fact you are not comfortable in doing so.

It is very easy however, for one to lose track of their aims and ambitions and follow in the path of others. This happens when instead of focusing on ourselves and ambitions we rather compare ourselves with others. We forget each of us has been created differently to fulfil a unique purpose in life and for whatever purpose we have been created, God has equipped us with special abilities. Of course, no two people created by God have the same abilities and capabilities. We all are unique in what we can do and although we may share some similarities with others, we are not and cannot be the same in everything we do. We may feel we do not measure up in our abilities to that of others around us when we compare ourselves to them. However, doing so will only lead to frustration and in some cases anxiety if we fail to run at our own pace.

Think about it this way. If we all see ourselves as parts of a big puzzle in that we all have different roles to play to make the puzzle complete we will better appreciate doing things at our own pace. The time it will take to move a piece of a puzzle to the base, might be less compared to what it will take to move another piece to the top. But then, each piece would have added up to making the puzzle complete if they fitted together as they should. If we refuse to run at our own pace, we will end up with inferior outcomes to what is expected of us.

It is okay to go an extra mile in order to achieve set goals and there is nothing wrong with stretching one's capacity for the same purpose. However, doing things to the extreme has its own disadvantages. It can lead to poor and undesirable outcomes. It also becomes a wrong thing if someone stretches their capacity in order to compete with someone else's achievement. When we do things at our own pace, we avoid having to overstretch our capabilities and work in the best way to achieve the expected outcomes. This gives us the reward of success and brings us contentment.

We read in this chapter that having assessed the strength and capabilities of the young children and the fact that some of the flocks and herds had their young, Jacob thought it wise for them to follow Esau and his troops at their own pace and meet up at Seir as they could not run at the same pace as them. Doing so ensured their safety as well as enabling them to achieve their aims. They each met up at Seir, although they travelled at different paces: their own pace. More so, they were able to accomplish their own goals which is important.

As mentioned earlier, the pressure we sometimes feel when we want to match up with other people's lives, we see around us could cause us to lose focus and prevent us from achieving our goals in life. However, when we learn to run at our own pace, we achieve better results.

Would you rather run at a pace you are comfortable with to ensure you do not burnout while working towards achieving your goals?

CHAPTER QUESTIONS

&

THEMES FOR THOUGHT

- What could be your gains if you stay focused and concentrate on what you are capable of?
- What are some of the dangers of always comparing yourself with other people?
- What would you do if you felt pressured by someone else's achievement?

YOU CAN SUMMARISE YOUR THOUGHTS

YOU CAN REVISIT YOUR THOUGHTS

CHAPTER 34

SELF-CONTROL

"Now Dinah, the daughter Leah had borne to Jacob, went out to visit the women of the land. When Shechem son of Hamor the Hivite, the ruler of that area, saw her, he took her and raped her." (NIV)

Genesis 34:1-2

MESSAGE AND LEARNING

The world we live in offers a craving for physical pleasure (1 John 2: 16-17). The lustful desires of the flesh, the cravings for the things we see, itching ears always seeking out messages that destroy one's lifestyle and uncontrollable tongues that utter destructive words, all lead to ruin and ultimately death. Life is such that, if we do not learn to constrain ourselves from saying or acting in ways which are unacceptable, or learn to say no to certain things, we will find ourselves in trouble all the time. The Christian bible therefore teaches us to control ourselves and gives examples of certain aspects of life in which we must control ourselves. One of these is learning to hold our tongues from evil and our lips from telling lies, if we love our lives and desire to see many good days. Another example is controlling our temper when provoked as not doing so could lead to anger and result in evil doing. Much the same we are to control ourselves in order not to involve ourselves in practices such as committing sexual perversion (pre-marital sex, lesbianism, gay practices), smoking, drunkenness and the like, all of which destroy our lives. Yet many are lured into and give in to such cravings and desires that lead to wrongdoings all because of a lack of self-control.

Two acts of a lack of self-control are presented in this chapter. One of which is an inability to control the lustful sexual desires of the flesh. Shechem, saw Dinah and was attracted to her. He loved her and he longed to have her as his wife. But he could not control his sexual desires for Dinah and went ahead and raped her. He could have constrained himself until he had sought her hand in marriage before going ahead to rape her. But his inability to constrain himself from that desire and rather doing the right thing, led him away from the ultimate desire of having Dinah as his wife. Thus, he did not get to marry Dinah in the first place. Furthermore, his lack of self-control led to his death and that of all the men of the town including his father.

We also learn that two of Dinah's brothers Simeon and Levi, failed to control their anger as a result of Shechem's actions and took matters into their own hands, killing the men in the town. By acting in their anger and frustration of what had happened, they also had to pay for what they did. Their actions brought disgrace upon their father and lead to the pronunciation of a curse on them by their father Jacob at a time when he should have blessed them.

Through a lack of self-control many have said things that have destroyed lives and relationships and caused regrets, shame and disgrace.

Have there been times when you were unable to control your temper and have acted in a way or said something and now wished you had not done it or wished you could take back those words? Have you ever failed to control your cravings for something (for instance smoking, drinking alcohol or overeating) and later on regret doing it? What choices are you making from now on? A choice to control yourself or not?

CHAPTER QUESTIONS

&

THEMES FOR THOUGHT

- Is there anything you said or did that actually put you in trouble and if yes, what do you think you ought to have done in order to have avoided such trouble?
- Is there an area in your life that you have realised needs self-control?

YOU CAN SUMMARISE YOUR THOUGHTS

YOU CAN REVISIT YOUR THOUGHTS

CHAPTER 35

SHOWING GRATITUDE TO GOD

So, Jacob told everyone in his household, "Get rid of all your pagan idols, purify yourselves, and put on clean clothing. We are now going to Bethel, where I will build an altar to the God who answered my prayers when I was in distress. He has been with me wherever I have gone." (NLT)
Genesis 35:2&3

MESSAGE AND LEARNING

I wonder why most of us cannot forget the wrongdoings done to us by others. Yet, we so easily forget the kindness shown to us, let alone remember to show our gratitude for them. Gratitude is a quality exhibited through readiness to show an appreciation for things done for a person, no matter what the extent or magnitude of the kindness shown to them. It comprises of an act of recognition, acknowledgement and the return of kindness. Recognition in the sense that, the person who is grateful, recognises or identifies what has been done to them or for them, or an encounter they have experienced. They then acknowledge the fact that, they encountered that experience or received the kindness shown to them from someone, which is a source. The only way gratitude can be shown, is through an act of returning kindness received either through words or deeds. Jacob portrayed these three things; this was his way of showing gratitude to God.

Firstly, we find a list of things Jacob identifies or recognises has been done for him. He knew exactly what God had done for him; he thought of them and was able to name them one by one. Twice, he had experienced God in a supernatural way at Bethel. That is, when he was running away from his brother Esau to Paddan- Aran and on his return. Both encounters, God had blessed him. He was blessed in land and his seeds were going to be greatly multiplied. Also, his name was changed from Jacob (a supplanter) to Israel (a nation). Instead of wrongfully seizing what belonged to another and holding their place in the past, he was now blessed in all things and had no need of using illegitimate means to get the things that did not belong to him. Furthermore, his prayers were answered in his time of distress. He also had a companion who stayed with him wherever he went. More so, he and his household received God's protection, and no one was able to attack or harm them.

The other thing we realise is that he acknowledges the Lord God, as the source of everything he had. He is the source to the life he lived, his children, his wealth, his protection and his future.

Thirdly, we gather from the passage that he was quick to give in return the kindness that was shown to him. He readily gave what he thought was befitting to God. Although what he had given could not measure up to the worth of what was given to him by God, he gave the best he could give to show his appreciation. God does so much more for us than we can ever repay him for. However, showing our gratitude in a kind way is a way of showing others how much he has done for us and telling of his goodness. When we fail to make known his goodness to others, by keeping what he has done for us to ourselves and not expressing how we feel about it in words or deeds, we are ungrateful in our ways. Jacob showed gratitude by ensuring everyone in his household renewed their relationship with God by destroying their idols, the things they saw as the biggest in their lives and placed more value on them than God. They also had to make a journey, an act in view of going to express their gratitude, no matter the difficulties that befell them or the distractions encountered on the way. In addition to this, he built an altar unto the Lord without focusing on the loss to him but rather considering God's worth, which is an act of worship. These are some of the ways in which he chose to express his gratitude to God. But there are similar and other ways by which we too can show our gratitude to God. These include, thanksgiving, praise, the giving of testimonies and through our offerings unto God.

Simply put, a grateful heart is a joyful or happy heart. When we are grateful to people for the things they have done for us, we are eager to show it through our actions for them to know we truly are grateful. In this way, a heart filled with gratitude radiates the happiness it has experienced towards the one from whom kindness has been received. The least way in which such kindness returns from such a grateful heart, is by doing what will make the other person happy as well. When we truly are grateful to God for the things, he has done for us, we return our kindness through our actions by doing things that will not cause him hurt but rather make him happy. Primarily, this can be achieved by doing God's will. That is, the repenting of our sins and not repeating them anymore. We realise from the passage that Jacob told everyone in his household to destroy their idols, wash themselves and put on clean clothing. This meant that, he and his entire household had repented their sins, had fully separated themselves from their past sinful ways and had received the new ways of God on how to live from then onwards. That is gratitude!

Expressing gratitude to God is one of the ways of accessing his favour. This is also portrayed in the passage in that, every time Jacob showed gratitude, God did a new thing in his life. It also means that ingratitude or ungratefulness has been robbing many people of the favour of God. As well as that, every favour you fail to appreciate God for depreciates, just as every blessing whose source you fail to acknowledge disappears. By not showing our gratitude to God therefore, we miss out on a lot of blessings which he has made available to us.

As already mentioned in the earlier paragraph one of the ways by which people fail to show gratitude is through forgetfulness. When they enjoy the kindness, they have received and forget that it had a source and that what they received did not just show up out of nowhere. Besides forgetfulness is pride, in that others refuse to recognise the source and live with a false belief that any kindness shown them was as a result of their own making. They believe all has been achieved through their own effort, wisdom, strength and other abilities, which is deception. All these rob us of many of God's continual blessings. If we decide to let go of them, we can be certain of receiving every blessing meant for us.

Has God done something for you, that you should be grateful for? Do you regard him as your source?
Is there anything you are holding onto that you need to let go of, for God to take his rightful place in your life? Will you make a choice to show gratitude for all of God's benefits towards you?

CHAPTER QUESTIONS

&

THEMES FOR THOUGHT

- Do you have the habit of showing gratitude to God or to people who show you kindness?
- How do you personally show gratitude to God?
- Do you think going to church to worship God could be a way of showing gratitude to him?

YOU CAN SUMMARISE YOUR THOUGHTS

YOU CAN REVISIT YOUR THOUGHTS

CHAPTER 36

MOVING ON IN LIFE

Esau took his wives, his children, and his entire household, along with his livestock and cattle—all the wealth he had acquired in the land of Canaan—and moved away from his brother, Jacob. There was not enough land to support them both because of all the livestock and possessions they had acquired. So, Esau (also known as Edom) settled in the hill country of Seir. (NLT)

Genesis 36: 6-8

MESSAGE AND LEARNING

At certain times in our lives, we find ourselves staying too long at a place, when we should in fact be progressing forward with our lives. Sometimes we get comfortable with our routines and are just not bothered to move on in life. Many a times, we gain much comfort in the things or situations around us to such an extent that the thought of moving on is simply not an option. Other times, it is not so much about the comfort we enjoy (as most of us are not comfortable in the state at which we find ourselves in) but the fact that we feel a sense of security where we are, and we would rather stay there and not move on. The fear of the unknown, uncertainty of the future, stumbling blocks, hindrances and challenges we might encounter and the fear of failing in life all serve as deterrents to many causing them not to move on in life. For this reason, most people are held back in life and miss out on life changing opportunities because they fear change.

It is understandable if people do not move on in life when it is not the right time to do so or if God asks them to stay on for a reason. But if all situations prove that we have dwelt too long at a place and there is a need to do so, it is necessary we gather the courage, trust in God for the uncertainties that are ahead and move on without question. The earth is in constant motion and so is everything else. We therefore have to keep with it and move on when there is the need to do so. Otherwise, we fall behind and miss out on the many wonderful opportunities ahead of us. Also, just as running water goes stale and breeds disease causing agents when left stagnant, we too can outgrow specific circumstances if we do not move on when we should, and this may cause problems in the future.

We learn from previous chapters that Jacob returned to Mamre where his father Isaac and his brother Esau lived. He returned with his family and all he had acquired. But we are told in this chapter that his brother Esau had also gained a lot of wealth on the land to an extent that the land could not support them both. Now, just pause and think for a moment about the fact that Esau unlike Jacob had lived in the land of Mamre all his life. He had made friends, married, raised his children and had worked there. He must have been comfortable living there or perhaps found security in the things he did there and the place itself. For him to move on therefore, must have not been an easy thing for him to do. More so, considering that he was already doing well on the land and that his brother Jacob had come to join him at a later time, it would have been much easier if he had stayed, and Jacob moved on instead. But, he had to move on.

In circumstances where we outgrow situations, for instance, if one gains more experience in a particular job and can progress to a role where such an experience can be better utilised or if one's vision grows bigger than what it used to be in life, there is the need to broader our horizons.

Do you think it is time to move on in terms of where you currently are in your education, career, ministry or wherever you are in life? Pause in life, take stock and move on if it is the right time to do so.

CHAPTER QUESTIONS

&

THEMES FOR THOUGHT

- What are some of the factors that can discourage people from moving on in life?
- What one thing will you consider if you should make a move from where you are presently?

YOU CAN SUMMARISE YOUR THOUGHTS

YOU CAN REVISIT YOUR THOUGHTS

CHAPTER 37

HATRED

One-night Joseph had a dream, and when he told his brothers about it, they hated him more than ever. "Listen to this dream," he said. "We were out in the field, tying up bundles of grain. Suddenly my bundle stood up, and your bundles all gathered around and bowed low before mine!" His brothers responded, "So you think you will be our king, do you? Do you actually think you will reign over us?" And they hated him all the more because of his dreams and the way he talked about them. (NLT)

Genesis 37: 5-8

MESSAGE AND LEARNING

The Collins dictionary describes hatred as an extreme dislike for something or someone. Surprisingly, some people hate others without a cause. Others hate as a response to what has been done to them. For instance, if a person's life, property or relationship is destroyed by another, this could hurt them so much to result in hatred for that person. Most people also hate others out of jealousy or envy. The fact that, they have identified a blessing upon someone's life or perceived where they could be in the near future could make them hate that person. In other words, the person who hates, feels the other person is better than they are in a way or wants something the other person has got that they have not got. There are others who might not necessarily hate that person but rather what they do. However, this could lead to hatred for that person after some time if this continues and measures are not taken to stop it. Bitterness, jealousy and envy, therefore, can all lead to hatred if not dealt with effectively.

A person who lives with hatred can do wrong through their thoughts, actions and words. Out of hatred people go on to tell lies about the people they hate to destroy their reputation, lives or relationships. Also, some wish the person they hate could lose what they have. Others also end up physically torturing those they hate and sometimes do so to an extent that lives can be lost in the cause of time. Yet, by hating other people and allowing this extreme emotion to control us, we could end up destroying our own lives. Hatred has led many to part company with their destiny helpers, these people who were meant to help them fulfil their purpose in life. According to Abuelaish and Arya (2017), hatred can endanger a person's health. Some people, as a result of hating others have ended up with poor mental health such as stress, anxiety and depression and also cardiovascular disease such as hypertension and arrhythmias: some of which have resulted in death. In some cases, it has led to broken relationships which cannot be restored.

We learn from this chapter that Joseph's brothers hated him. Although, the bible explicitly tells us one of the reasons they hated him was as a result of their father's love for him. It could also be because Joseph was an obedient loving child and sought to do whatever pleased his father. We can infer this from the fact that, the bible tells us he brings his father the evil reports of his brothers: things they did which he knew were wrong and their father would not like any of the things they did, but they did them anyway. By seeking to please his father, Joseph would have earned a degree of his father's affection compared to what they would have, and this made them hate him. Additionally, they hated him for his dreams. The fact that they knew he had a great future ahead of him and that they will at some point in time have to submit to him, made them hate him even more. For hatred, Joseph's brothers could not say any kind words to him. Besides that, they did not consider his kindness of willingly accepting to go and see how they and the flocks fared but rather sort to pay him back with hatred for the kindness he had shown to them. As well as that, they sat down to eat, not burdened with the fact that their brother, Joseph was in a state of discomfort, in the pit for the same reason. They saw his terror and anguish and heard his pleadings but did not listen nor care. Furthermore, they chose to part company with their brother over the relationship they once enjoyed with him and decided to sell him into slavery, because they hated him, not knowing he was later going to be a saviour to them.

We read from later chapters that through hatred they acted in a way that brought shame on them. Also, they had to live with a guilty conscience even after they had been forgiven by Joseph due to what they did to him out of the hatred they had for him. They also lived in fear that Joseph would pay them back for what they did to him, hence they could not relate to him as closely as they should have done.

A way through which hatred can be avoided is through forgiveness. When we easily forgive those who hurt us, the pain or bitterness caused to us by what has been done to us does not grow into hatred. Additionally, we can avoid hatred when we celebrate what others have that we have not got, particularly, if we want it too. By celebrating what others have that we want, we get an urge to work harder and through hard work can achieve it. Also, we are humbled, through our act of celebrating others. This allows us to freely ask for guidance from those who have what we admire in order to know the direction in which we ought to go to achieve our aim. It also encourages free sharing of ideas, instructions, guidance and other resources on the part of the person who has what we admire. Thereby, making it easier for us to achieve the same or even better aims and goals in life.

Would you rather not hate others and get to where you ought to be in life or not?

CHAPTER QUESTIONS

&

THEMES FOR THOUGHT

- What must we do in order not to develop hatred for others?
- What are some of the things that people who hate other people could do to them?
- State and explain three things that could provoke hatred.
- What one thing can you do to avoid the temptation of you hating someone else?

YOU CAN SUMMARISE YOUR THOUGHTS

YOU CAN REVISIT YOUR THOUGHTS

CHAPTER 38

JUDGING OTHERS

About three months later, Judah was told, "Tamar, your daughter-in-law, has acted like a prostitute. And now, because of this, she's pregnant." "Bring her out and let her be burned!" Judah demanded. (NIV)

Genesis 38: 24

MESSAGE AND LEARNING

A saying in the bible teaches us that it is easier for us to remove the plank in our eyes to aid us to see better in order to help take the speck out of the eyes of others. Yet, we are always so eager to point out the faults of others when in actual fact we are worse off in the same or similar ways because we are turning a blind eye to our own wrong doings. Most often we judge without knowing the whole story or the reason behind why the other person might have acted in the way they did. Besides this, we are not in any way in a position to judge others, bearing in mind that God is the only lawgiver hence, he is the only one that can judge. Additionally, we also, will someday be judged for our wrong motives and actions like them.

We draw from this chapter lessons on why we should not judge others. We learn that Judah was quick to judge Tamar for her act of prostitution and issued a punishment for her. Little did he know that the punishment is equally fit for him, as he played the same part in the act of prostitution as Tamar did. They equally played a part in the act but for the fact that he could hide his acts, thinking he would never be found out, while Tamar could not because her pregnancy gave her away. He was quick to judge her and went ahead to issue a punishment for her. Here is the case in which it would have been fair to have him burned as well, as he together with Tamar committed the act of prostitution.

In the first instance, Judah lied to his daughter in-law Tamar by not keeping his promise. He knew very well he was not going to allow his son Shelah to marry her but went ahead to give that promise. Besides this, he told Tamar not to marry again and to remain a widow until Shelah was old enough to marry her when in fact Tamar could have remarried. However, when Shelah had grown up and was ready for marriage Judah did not send for Tamar to marry him knowing Tamar was still waiting to get married again after her time of mourning was over. In addition, he went ahead to sleep with Tamar thinking she was a prostitute, an act which he knew was wrong and would bring shame upon him if he was to be found out and deserved a similar punishment. He did everything he could in his power to avoid being found out for this act. However, despite him trying to cover his shame, for an act he committed together with Tamar, he was eager to expose her act of prostitution and to have her burnt for the same indecent act he committed.

If we study carefully the acts of both Judah and Tamar, we get to find out that Judah had done more wrong compared to Tamar. Also, that, they were both involved in the same act of prostitution for which he wanted Tamar punished for. Why then, was he quick to judge her? Who are we to judge others knowing very well there is only one lawgiver and judge? We forget that it is only right for one who knows no sin to be able to judge others. The opposite being fair (that is, it would be wrong for us to judge others when we ourselves are committing the same or similar acts). God alone is righteous in all his ways. He alone can save and destroy. Hence why, he alone has the power to judge. Yet, he is slow to judge us for our motives and deeds while we are quick at judging others. The bible teaches us that the same measure we use to judge others will be used to judge us when we are judgemental. Hence why, we should not be quick to judge others.

Judging others stems from one or more of the following. The first being self-righteousness. When we see ourselves as having no sin and that we are right in all our ways forgetting that this attitude in itself is sin. If we are to remember, however, that in us is no good thing and that all the right things we do are as a result of God's influence on us and if God was to allow us to do whatever we chose to do, we would have fallen flat on our face in disgrace, we would never at any point see ourselves in a position to judge others. With this in mind, we will act in ways as to not be too quick to judge others.

Secondly, we are likely to judge others when we compare ourselves to them rather than compare ourselves to Jesus Christ, who should be our standard. This is true in the sense that, we could find ourselves better than others in some ways but not all ways. That is, we would have been able to cut ourselves from some sinful acts which they still find themselves doing. But then, when we get to know that they also probably do not do certain things we enjoy doing which the bible calls sin, we come to a realisation that we are actually no better than they are and that we are just equally as bad as we think they are but in other ways. It is only when we compare ourselves to Jesus Christ who knew no sin that we conclude that we are worse people than we actually thought we were. Coming to this realisation helps us see the need not to judge others, knowing well that they, just like us, need pardoning for all the wrong deeds. Also, just as we need help to enable us to live the right way, they in a likewise manner, will benefit from help given to them. Hence, rather than judging them, it would be right if we could help them out of the situation, we consider to be wrong.

Thirdly, judging others stems from a spirit of criticism. Here, we find this group of people finding faults with all or most things done by others when in fact what is being portrayed might not have been wrong in the first place.

Rather than judging others, it will be wise if we could examine ourselves and work on the things, we identify in our own lives that will make others stumble should they follow suit in those ways. Also, by helping those who are less fortunate in gaining knowledge through our acts of right deeds, we too could help them live in a way we are all expected to live. This will ensure we all live the right way thereby leaving no room for judgmental acts.

Will you be willing to help others not to falter in their ways by doing the right things rather than be judgemental in your ways?

CHAPTER QUESTIONS

&

THEMES FOR THOUGHT

- Why do you think it is wrong to judge others?
- How will you feel if others constantly pick on the things, you do wrong or are less good at, without helping you to overcome these weaknesses?
- Why do you think it is wrong to judge others?
- Is there anything you must deal with in your life in order not to be judgemental of other people?

YOU CAN SUMMARISE YOUR THOUGHTS

YOU CAN REVISIT YOUR THOUGHT

CHAPTER 39

FAITHFUL SERVICE

The Lord was with Joseph, so he succeeded in everything he did as he served in the home of his Egyptian master. Potiphar noticed this and realized that the Lord was with Joseph, giving him success in everything he did. This pleased Potiphar, so he soon made Joseph his personal attendant. He put him in charge of his entire household and everything he owned. (NLT)

Genesis 39: 2-4

MESSAGE AND LEARNING

Service is an act of working or doing something for someone else. One can serve in several ways and at different places. But in whichever way we choose to serve, it is important we do it faithfully. Many people naturally find themselves doing things effortlessly for those they love no matter how tedious the task they perform may be. However, it takes more effort both mentally and physically when the same task must be performed if there is a dislike for the person we serve under or if we do not particularly get on well with them.

One reason for this could be that, whilst we should be serving in a way to please God, we would rather seek the approval of men in the things we do and look forward to being rewarded by them. This impacts on the way we serve in that, if we do not receive approval or praise for what we do, we tend not to do them again. Our attitude towards the things we do and how we do them will however be different and more rewarding if we do them unto God. This is because God is the one who blesses the works of our hands, particularly when we do them faithfully. Faithfully in the sense that, things are done in the way they should be done, with diligence and in a consistent manner continually.

Also, when we serve faithfully in the things we do, not just once but in continuous service, we get better each time at them. We reap the rewards of our faithful service. Of course, the things we do best at, might go unnoticed if done as a one-off. However, with an act of continual, faithful service, there is less likelihood of what we do going unnoticed. Also, by faithfully serving in whatever capacity we find ourselves in, the gifts, abilities, effort and time God has given to us are put to good use. This glorifies God and causes him to bless us. His blessings can come to us in diverse ways. Sometimes, we receive these blessings in the form of favour, promotion, financial freedom, good health and long life.

Joseph faithfully served his master Potiphar until he became his favourite. He must certainly have met other servants in Potiphar's house who would have been serving in different capacities. But as already mentioned we all do not serve in the same way and have different attitudes towards the things we do and the way in which we do them. Joseph could have allowed himself to have been influenced by the way the others served and gotten similar rewards to them. However, he chose to faithfully serve his master Potiphar as though he was serving God. For this reason, God was pleased with him, was with him and gave him success in all he did. Since God's blessings attract people's attention, Potiphar noticed Joseph succeeded in all he did and put Joseph in charge of his entire household. Joseph must have shown Potiphar respect and done things in a way to attract his attention and earn his favour. Probably, he served in the same way both in Potiphar's presence and absence and much as others would have noticed it, God who sees all things saw it all. Thereby, rewarded Joseph's act of faithful service.

We however know that it is not just others and God who notice what we do and the success that comes with it, but the devil does also. Yet his intentions are always to steal, kill and destroy our successes. He does this by using ways to lure us into doing things that cause us to lose all we have worked hard for. In Joseph's case, the devil tried using Potiphar's wife as a means to destroy his success. He caused her to desire Joseph and wanted him to sleep with her. Yet, Joseph remained faithful in his service, in that although he was put in charge of everything Potiphar owned, he knew where the power given to him ended, he knew his limits. Most people, however, fail to acknowledge the boundaries within which they are to work when power is entrusted to them and tread beyond these limits. Some serve in places and take things that do not belong to them but for it being under their care and power still do. Others take advantage of their subordinates and mistreat them in ways they choose to, when really, they should be helping them. While some just do not care about the outcomes and implications of the actions they take. If their actions prevent the growth of the organisation they serve in, they still go ahead and do them anyway. Joseph could have gone ahead and slept with Potiphar's wife and kept it a secret between the two of them, but he remained faithful and loyal as servant to Potiphar and resisted the temptation. He did that bearing in mind that although no one could have found out about his betrayal God would have known and punished him accordingly. This way he served his master and God simultaneously.

However, as already stated when you are in a faithful service you do not stop whatever you are doing whether you get praise for it or not, or there is an uplifting or not.

We have learnt from this chapter that, if we want to be faithful in our service, we must do it diligently, consistently and continually, while respecting others and with an aim to please God.

Would you rather serve faithfully or not?

CHAPTER QUESTIONS

&

THEMES FOR THOUGHT

- In what way will you choose to serve your family?
- What are some of the rewards we receive for serving faithfully?

YOU CAN SUMMARISE YOUR THOUGHTS

YOU CAN REVISIT YOUR THOUGHTS

CHAPTER 40

PUTTING YOUR GIFT TO USE

"This is what it means," Joseph said to him. "The three branches are three days. Within three days Pharaoh will lift up your head and restore you to your position, and you will put Pharaoh's cup in his hand, just as you used to do when you were his cupbearer." (NIV)

Genesis 40: 12&13

MESSAGE AND LEARNING

God has given each one of us gifts. Gifts fit for the purpose for which we were each created, regardless of our age, gender, colour and background. We, however, do not get to choose the gifts given us but we receive them according to what will help us fulfil our destinies. Although we might feel our gift is insignificant or that we probably have fewer gifts as compared to what others have, it is important that we do not despise them or envy others because of the gifts they received. Rather, it is vital we discover our gifts, appreciate them, develop them and put them to good use, so they can benefit us and others while giving glory to God.

When we use them well to serve each other, it brings us fulfilment in life and gives glory to God. In the sense that, God created each of us for a purpose. He had a plan and a reason for our existence in life. He knew what each of us will be capable of doing having the right resources, prior to creating us. More so, he created us to meet a need he had on earth knowing perfectly well we can meet that need should he equip us well. So, he created us for a purpose and knowing the purpose for which he created us, has equipped each of us with the right gifts so we can accomplish these purposes with ease and gain satisfaction while at the same time fulfilling his purpose and making him happy.

On the other hand, we do not get to fulfil the purpose for which we were created if we do not put the gifts given to us to good use. This is because work that needs doing is left undone, when in fact, it should be done as has been assigned to us, together with all the necessary requirements needed to do it. Besides this, when the gifts given to us are not put to good use, they lay idle and become unprofitable to us, to others and to God when in actual fact it has been given to us for our benefit and that of others. This does not bring glory to God considering we, as well as others suffer because of our failure in putting our gifts to good use.

A lot of people are struggling in life because they are not paying attention to God's gift to them. They have either left behind the one thing that will make way for their success while chasing after the wind, hence, concentrating on others. While some are unaware of God's gift to them and have not bothered to discover it, others have been led astray by focussing on the gifts of others and what they are doing with them.

Joseph was gifted with dreams and was well known for them to the extent that his brothers named him the dreamer. He also enjoyed sharing his dreams with others and told them to such an extent that the interpretation of his dreams stood out vividly each time he did. He was good at it. Although he was hated because of his dreams, and there were hindrances to stop him, it did not stop him from dreaming more, neither did it stop him from sharing his dreams. Gradually, the dreamer had become an interpreter of dreams. His gift has been developed. From being a dreamer and narrator of dreams, he could now interpret the dreams of others. He saw the essence of meeting the needs of others through interpretation of their dreams. This made way for him in the presence of Pharaoh the king of Egypt. Certainly, a man's gift opens doors for him and brings him before great men as said in the book of Proverbs. If he had left this gift idle and not put it to good use, he will not have risen to the position he was at. It could also have led to him and his family struggling through the years of the famine. God's promises of making the people of Israel a great nation in the land of Egypt, before bringing them back to Canaan would not have been fulfilled if he despised his gift. In our time, many have put their gifts to good use, and we benefit from them in many ways. For instance, Alexander Bell invented the telephone, to enable us to communicate with friends and family from far away. Furthermore, this also instigated mobile telecommunications in today's society. Another, invention was by John Peake Knight who invented the traffic lights to assist with our safe travels on the roads today. If these people had not used their gifts, then our lives would have been so different and would have fallen short of these things.

Are you being called names given to you, as a result of the things you are good at? Have you noticed particular things you excel in and get praise for each time you do them? Are you hated or envied for things you do to help others when rather they should have earned your praise? Is there anything you enjoy doing and find yourself doing effortlessly regardless of the circumstances surrounding you? Are there things you find yourself getting angry about, when you see people doing them any way when they sure could do it better? All these are indications of you possessing the ability to excel in them. They are a means through which you can discover your gifts. If you answer yes to any of these, that should more than likely be the gift that God has given you.

Once you have discovered your gift however, you will have to develop it. You can either do this by reading and getting more knowledge and information about it, through schooling or a vocation, to mention but a few.

It is important to remember that besides others suffering the consequences of your failure of putting your gift to good use, you bear the most consequences. It impacts negatively on your life in this world and the next as you become useless to yourself, to others and to God.

Would you rather put your gift to good use or not?

CHAPTER QUESTIONS

&

THEMES FOR THOUGHT

- Mention the names of three people whose gifts have brought benefits to the world?
- Why do you think we each have gifts and talents?
- In what ways can you develop your gifts or talents?

YOU CAN SUMMARISE YOUR THOUGHTS

YOU CAN REVISIT YOUR THOUGHTS

CHAPTER 41

SAVING MENTALITY

Therefore, Pharaoh should find an intelligent and wise man and put him in charge of the entire land of Egypt. Then Pharaoh should appoint supervisors over the land and let them collect one-fifth of all the crops during the seven good years. Have them gather all the food produced in the good years that are just ahead and bring it to Pharaoh's storehouses. Store it away, and guard it so there will be food in the cities. That way there will be enough to eat when the seven years of famine come to the land of Egypt. Otherwise, this famine will destroy the land."

Genesis 41: 33-36

MESSAGE AND LEARNING

"While the earth remained, seedtime and harvest, and cold and heat, and summer and winter, and day and night shall not cease (Genesis 8:22 KJV)". There will be great times just as there will be challenging times. Hence, the need for us to ensure in our good times, we plan and make provisions for the future. The ant is wise in this sense, in that neither having an overseer or ruler, knows how to gather food in times of plenty and store its provisions in the summer when conditions are favourable for it to work. This ensures it has enough supply come wintertime when the weather is not conducive for it.

God in his wisdom has made known to us the many ways through which we can save so we do not run out of supplies. He created seed bearing plants and trees that grew seeds bearing fruits. This was to ensure the existence of the trees as their seeds will then produce the kinds of plants and trees from which they came. Consider what would happen if we ate the fruit as well as the seeds, there will be no seeds for planting and hence no expectation of a harvest when it should be in season. This will mean a lack when indeed there should be plenty of provisions for the whole time ahead. Also, by saving the seeds we ensure continual existence of the created species.

God, through nature, therefore teaches us how we can save the things he has given us so that we continually have supplies of the seeds and fruits we need to survive. If we however do not have a saving mentality, we lose out and might end up struggling to make ends meet when in fact we should be having a constant source of supply for our needs. In a way, people who save have foresight. They live with an ambition of not having to depend on others for their needs, hence plan ahead of time.

This chapter teaches us the need to save. The need to remember there are portions of what we receive that are not for present use but allow for future provisions. The need not to waste what we have in our times of abundance, remembering the future is full of uncertainties.

Joseph after interpreting Pharaoh's dream suggested a saving plan in which part of the produce of the land of Egypt during the seven plentiful years will be stored as reserve for the land against the seven years of famine. This was to ensure continuous supply even in the times of famine so none would perish as a result of it. He had a saving mentality and saved in the wisest way he could in his time.

What then is the wisest way in which one could save in our time?

We find out the world we live in presents us with different ways in which we can save. While the majority believe in investing the extra money they have in a savings account of a bank, others would rather invest in antiques, collectibles or properties. Some also think it wise to invest in bonds, stocks, shares and equities. Whatever of these ways and others not mentioned here that you feel conversant to use is your decision to make as long as you have weighed your options and found what suits you best. In whatever case, it is good if we can invest in our future in whatever way, we can. The only concern is, there are still uncertainties with each of these ways of investments and there will always be, as no man can have ultimate control over the challenges that surround them.

There, however, exists other ways of investment which come with more benefits and with no risks associated, which should have greater prominence in our lives but which most of us pay little or no attention to when it comes to savings. Jesus tells us in the book of Luke, to invest in the heavens which fails not, where moths cannot destroy and thieves' approach. We can do this by investing in the lives of others, giving to the needy and giving to promote the work of the kingdom of God through tithes and offerings, just to mention a few. By doing this, we would not only have saved the lives of others but also in the kingdom of God, where we can be certain of withdrawing what we have saved when we need it the most. Knowing that, whenever we give to the needy, we lend to God. Also, whatever we have given to God is saved for us and will be given to us in our times of need through diverse ways. More so, we not only get the same amount we have given out but a measure, proportionate to and greater than what we had given in the first place.

It is vital therefore that in planning ways in which we save, we consider some of these ways of investment, as well as investing in the kingdom of God, so we have the assurance of supplies during difficult times.

Would you choose to have a saving mentality from now on?

CHAPTER QUESTIONS

&

THEMES FOR THOUGHT

- Why is it important to save?
- What Avenue will you choose to save your money towards any future eventualities?

YOU CAN SUMMARISE YOUR THOUGHTS

YOU CAN REVISIT YOUR THOUGHTS

CHAPTER 42

LEARNING FROM PAST MISTAKES

Jacob wouldn't let Joseph's younger brother, Benjamin, go with them, however, for fear some harm might come to him.

Genesis 42:4

But Jacob replied, "My son will not go down with you, for his brother Joseph is dead, and he alone is all that is left of his mother's children. If anything should happen to him, you would bring my grey head down to the grave in deep sorrow.

Genesis 42: 38

MESSAGE AND LEARNING

No one ever plans a mistake in life. No matter how hard we try to avoid making mistakes, we find ourselves acting or making wrong or misguided decisions at certain stages of our lives which cause us regret. Some people make mistakes as a result of sheer curiosity. Also, by trying to find out things for themselves or experience what they have heard without learning lessons from others, some could end up making mistakes. When in fact, they could learn from the mistakes of others and avoid similar ones;

they rather go ahead in a way of experiencing things for themselves and end up making the same or similar mistakes. Others make mistakes because they lack sufficient information about the choices they make or are simply inexperienced in decisions they make or the things they do. Rather than being patient until they have acquired the much-needed information or experience before making sensitive choices, they go on to make them anyway and realise later, they have made a mistake. Some particularly the youth, allow their peers to influence choices they make and thereby make these errors of judgements. Peer pressure has been known to be a key factor leading to mistakes being made in this age group probably because it gives them a sense of belonging when they find themselves doing the things others do. Also, we are bound to make mistakes when we wrongly judge the end results of situations.

The mistakes we make can cause us much hurt and rid us of the things we desire most in life. Surprisingly, some of us end up making the same errors of judgement repeatedly facing similar circumstances. Other times, we repeat the same or similar mistakes and find ourselves regretting our actions and hurting even the more when we do not learn from past mistakes. This is because we do not learn from our mistakes, when in fact we should.

Notwithstanding, we can benefit from our mistakes when we choose to learn from them. We do not end up making the same mistakes should we make use of lessons gained from ones we have previously made. We also find out that, people who learn from their mistakes avoid many regrets as they are able to prevent further similar errors from happening. They become better people, in that they find better ways to deal with similar situations which led to a previous mistake and make wiser choices thereafter.

Having said this, we would be foolish then, if we continue making the same errors of judgement repeatedly. The book of Proverbs, likens a fool to a dog in that, it knows its vomit is not good but still returns to it. In a similar way, we could be foolish if we keep repeating the same mistakes over and over again in our lives when faced with similar circumstances. People who repeat the same mistakes are either unwilling to modify their concepts by refusing to yield to opinions other than theirs or are reluctant to change their attitudes and habits. They get excessively overindulged with their old ways and continue in them with no motive to change.

We can gather from this chapter that Jacob had learnt from the mistakes he made. He allowed his son Joseph to go and check on his half-brothers (the sons of his father's wives Bilhah and Zilpah) and now, realised he would see him no more. For this reason, he would not let Joseph's younger brother, Benjamin, go with his half-brothers, if he were to lose him too. Earlier in chapter 37 of the book of Genesis, we read that Jacob had sent Joseph (one of the sons born to him in his old age by Rachel) to go and check on his brothers who had been gone for too long a time to pasture their father's flock. However, Joseph did not return, and this made Jacob mourn deeply for him, many days without gaining comfort from anything anyone said. Much the same, Benjamin was loved in that; he was born to Jacob in his old age by the same woman, Rachel. He was the only child left born to Rachel and considering that Jacob lost Joseph when left to the company of his half-brothers, he would not let Benjamin go with them facing the same circumstances. He could lose Benjamin also in their company! Hence, he would not let him go with them. He must have carefully reflected on the past decisions he made, assessed the situation at hand, weighed the options he had and carefully considered the expected outcome of the choices at hand before deciding he was not going to allow Benjamin to go with them.

It is important therefore that we too take some time to reflect on these past mistakes and errors of judgement, consider the factors that led to them and put measures in place, so they are not repeated but rather, prevent them from occurring again in the future. We can do this by identifying the mistakes we have made. Then, carefully consider all the factors that we know may have contributed to them. Also, a detailed examination of the contributing factors that could be made to ensure the right measures are employed to avoid the same or similar mistakes from occurring again. Doing so will make us better people, as by avoiding these errors of judgement repeatedly we free ourselves from unwanted results and regrets, while achieving better expected outcomes.

What then are you likely to do when faced with similar situations and circumstances in which you previously made mistakes? Will you pause and reflect on ways in which you can avoid the same mistakes recurring or blindly repeat the same mistakes previously made? Will you be willing to learn from your past errors of judgement and avoid repeating them?

CHAPTER QUESTIONS

&

THEMES FOR THOUGHT

- Why is it important to learn from your past mistakes?
- What could be the result of refusing to learn from your past mistakes?

YOU CAN SUMMARISE YOUR THOUGHTS

YOU CAN REVISIT YOUR THOUGHTS

CHAPTER 43

HONESTY

"We beg your pardon, our lord," they said, "we came down here the first time to buy food. But at the place where we stopped for the night, we opened our sacks and each of us found his silver—the exact weight—in the mouth of his sack. So, we have brought it back with us." (NIV)

Genesis 43: 20-21

MESSAGE AND LEARNING

A way in which you can easily spot a dishonest person is through the act of telling lies. Thus, a dishonest character births a lying conduct. A person who is honest however, is one who always tells the truth even in difficult situations and gives frank and sincere opinions even if it sounds unpleasant or offends in some way.

Honesty sometimes comes with costs which many would rather avoid and hence end up being dishonest. Most often, in an attempt to avoid getting punished for an act, or for fear of being found guilty of an offence and hence losing the respect and trust previously enjoyed, people would rather be dishonest. Some are dishonest because they think in doing so, they can continue to retain a position of power they occupy. Others live in dishonesty in order to acquire things for themselves and have a much better life. Yet, no matter how well we try to hide the truth, it eventually comes out into the light at a point in time. If at all we are able to achieve our aims through being dishonest, the negative impact of our actions overrides all we are able to achieve. Thus, the consequences of being dishonest far outweigh that of being honest. In that, if one is found to be a dishonest person, people not only fail to trust them with similar things but also lose trust in them concerning other things. In addition, considering that unlike telling the truth which can only be the truth, a dishonest person punishes themselves by continuing to fabricate stories which are inconsistent in nature until they are eventually found out. Furthermore, dishonest people normally live with guilt and in constant fear of being found out. When you tell the truth, the truth is a real image of what really happened. Hence, it is much easier to relay the truth than to tell lies. When you tell lies you then have to tell more lies as you cannot remember the previous lies you have told. You then get found out and are put to shame because your dishonest act has come to light.

Here is the case in which Joseph's brothers find money they used to pay for grain they bought, returned in their sacks without their knowledge. They could have pretended they knew nothing about it and kept it as their money was collected when they bought the grain. This could have paid for a second lot of grain or met another need they had. They could have also returned part of it and pretended that was all that was returned to them and left the rest for themselves. However, although they had no knowledge of how the money got into their sacks and could have benefited from it, they returned it. It could have ruined their reputation and rendered them dishonest men if they decided to keep some or all of it. Also, they might not have been able to buy more grain if they have been found to be dishonest. On the other hand, the fact that they decided to return the money instead of keeping it, could have earned them the trust and gratitude of the household manager. Their act of returning what did not belong to them portrays their honesty in such an act.

Sometimes our words or actions give us away and allow others to know who we truly are. If people find out we are dishonest, it can lead to distrust, loss of reputation and a breakdown in relationships. It could also lead to a lack of confidence and security in oneself as they live in fear of being caught out all the time. While on the other hand, honesty, asides, giving the opposite of what has already been mentioned, can open many doors of opportunities for people.

If we are truly children of God, we should be honest in our ways as dishonesty comes from the devil and we should not tell lies as Satan is the father of all lies.

Would you rather be honest or dishonest?

CHAPTER QUESTIONS

&

THEMES FOR THOUGHT

- How will you identify a dishonest person?
- What could be the consequences of being dishonest?
- Trying to be honest in all situations comes at a cost. Do you agree with this statement or not?

YOU CAN SUMMARISE YOUR THOUGHTS

YOU CAN REVISIT YOUR THOUGHTS

CHAPTER 44

LEADERSHIP

"Then Judah stepped forward and said, "Please, my lord, let your servant say just one word to you. Please, do not be angry with me, even though you are as powerful as Pharaoh himself." (NLT)

-Genesis 44: 18

MESSAGE AND LEARNING

Most people want to be leaders, but it is not everyone who can be a leader. Certainly, some people must be led by others. There are born leaders and although one can be coached to be a leader, it is not an easy role to take on, as many struggle to lead others. Leaders are identified by their ability to get their team to follow their vision, ideas, instructions or recommendations. To achieve these however, they must have certain unique qualities. Some of which include commitment to the team, trustworthiness, good communication and interpersonal skills, just to mention a few.

Here in this chapter, we can identify certain qualities Judah displayed which identifies him as a born leader to his brothers. Firstly, we learn that Judah managed to persuade Jacob to allow Benjamin to go to Egypt with his brothers to buy grain, even though Jacob was unwilling to allow him to accompany them there. Had he not done so, they would not have been able to get more grain from Egypt. The ability to persuade others therefore to buy into one's ideas and suggestions is a key skill in good leadership. This is because not everyone being led will easily appreciate and embrace an idea, let alone act on it to effect a change. Hence why, the need to be able to persuade others in instances where there is a need to instigate a change. We read in chapter 37 of the book of Genesis that, Judah was able to convince his brothers into buying into his idea of selling Joseph to the Ishmaelite traders when in fact, they each had their own plans of what they wanted done to him. Here in this chapter, we learn that although Judah was not a leader to his father at the time but rather to his brothers, he managed to persuade his father into buying into the idea of allowing Benjamin to go to Egypt with them. We also learn that his ideas had to be communicated in a way to influence the decision Jacob made.

Judah was a good communicator. He used the right words while communicating with both Jacob and Joseph to put his message across in order to convince them both into doing what he wanted to be done. If he had failed in using the right words, presenting them in the right way, under the right circumstances, he would not have achieved his goals in both instances. Every leader leads a team to achieve a goal and in order to do so, it is vital that as a leader one can communicate effectively. This skill is essential to enable the leader to be able to present clearly the vision at hand, give the right information, in a simple to understand but convincing manner as to make others do what is required of them. Ineffective communication can however result in poor responses from the team being led, lead to less optimal delivery of tasks and result in unwanted outcomes.

Judah did not only persuade Jacob to buy into his idea but also, he displayed the quality of empathy towards Jacob. He did this by listening to the concerns Jacob had and used thoughtful words to answer questions he had. He also, reassured him of some positive outcomes that will be achieved if he allowed Benjamin go with them. For instance, the fact that he mentioned Benjamin's going with them will enable them to buy some food and prevent them from starving to death. Also, he was going to ensure Benjamin's safety should he accompany them, this might have advanced Jacob's interest concerning the idea and made him send Benjamin with them. When a leader is able to empathise with members in the team and listen to their concerns, it makes them feel they are cared for and that they are part of the team with regard to decisions being made and ensures any objections they might have regarding an idea or suggestion are listened to.

We also find out that Judah was willing to accept the responsibility of ensuring Benjamin returned to his father. This teaches us that leadership comes with responsibility. The responsibility of either performing tasks in a team or alone, in as much as individuals in a team will have their own responsibilities, the leader might have an added responsibility of ensuring things are done as required to achieve the required goals and outcomes of the team.

Leadership also comes with accountability and Judah was prepared to be held accountable should any harm come to Benjamin. Leaders are held accountable for outcomes. Particularly, in situations where potential consequences of not reaching desired results exist. They are the sole people to blame should the desired results not be achieved. For this reason, a good leader ensures all the necessary structures are put in place so that positive outcomes can be achieved. Knowing he will be held accountable should any harm come to Benjamin, Judah was willing to do everything possible to bring Benjamin back home.

We see in this chapter Judah's determination and desperation in ensuring Benjamin returned to his father while pleading with Joseph to let Benjamin go with his brothers. He was willing to stay in Egypt as a slave instead, so Benjamin could return to his father with his brothers. He had pledged to his father to take good care of Benjamin and knew he will be held accountable should anything happen to him.

Good leaders also take the initiative. Judah was the one who took the initiative to explain things to Joseph. Most people learn and act by watching and practicing desired behaviours in their leaders. If a leader takes the initiative with tasks that need to be performed, it encourages members to do the same and makes them work better at duties assigned to them. Everyone looks up to a leader to take the initiative and most people work better if they have a leader who takes the initiative in a task hence why this attribute is key to good leadership.

Also, Judah wanted to fulfil the promise he made to his father of bringing Benjamin back home safe and sound. The only way to make people feel comfortable around you and act upon the things you tell them is through trust. Honouring promises you make serves as evidence of your credibility and enables others to trust you knowing you will not let them down. It is vital therefore to honour promises you make as a leader as not doing so will make people lose their confidence or trust they have in you and subsequently impact negatively on future expected outcomes.

Having learnt about the qualities displayed by Judah as a leader in this chapter, we too can build on existing qualities and learn new skills to enable us to lead a team effectively should we be entrusted with such a role. Doing so will ensure we lead the team in the manner expected and achieve the desired outcomes.

Would you want to lead a team effectively if you are required to do so? If yes, will you build on existing qualities and learn new skills to enable you to be a good leader?

CHAPTER QUESTIONS

&

THEMES FOR THOUGHT

- Discuss five qualities of a good leader?
- Knowing the demands of being a leader, would you want to be one? If yes why, and if not why?
- How can one develop their leadership skills?
- Do you believe a leader should be able to think ahead and put measures in place towards unforeseen circumstances?

YOU CAN SUMMARISE YOUR THOUGHTS

YOU CAN REVISIT YOUR THOUGHTS

CHAPTER 45

FORGIVENESS

Weeping with joy, he embraced Benjamin, and Benjamin did the same. Then Joseph kissed each of his brothers and wept over them, and after that they began talking freely with him. (NLT)
Genesis 45: 14&15

MESSAGE AND LEARNING

I wonder if there is anyone who would want to relate with an enemy. Someone who hates you, always says unkind words to you and more so, one who has plans to harm you. It is obvious that most of us will relate to people who act kindly towards us, people who will want to help us achieve our dreams and ambitions, those who will make us feel a sense of happiness and hope when around us. We live in hope that once we have shown others acts of kindness, they will tend to feel, think and act in similar ways towards us. But this is not always the case. When we find ourselves showing love to someone, caring for them and are willing to sacrifice in ways for them but later realise they have evil intentions towards us or act in ways we do not expect, it can cause us much pain and hurt. In some instances, we may go to an extent of wanting to pay them back for the wrongs they did. But, Jesus teaches us to forgive others the wrongs they do to us, remembering that it is only in doing so that God will forgive us our wrongdoings. If we cannot forgive others what they do to us, then we cannot receive God's forgiveness.

Forgiveness requires our total deletion of the wrongs people do to us. Hence, it involves changing our mindset through our thoughts, words and deeds. This makes it pretty hard to forgive. In the first instance, thoughts about all the wrongs people do to us linger in our minds when we do not have intentions of forgiving others. Besides this, when we encounter similar situations that resulted in us getting hurt, it allows our hurting to grow into bitterness which makes it difficult for us to forget what has been done to us, hence, the need for forgiveness. When we are unable to control our thoughts and feelings, we find ourselves saying and acting in ways that harbour and nurture them until they grow out of hand and finally destroy the relationship we are in. Forgiveness can be daunting but gives relief, restoration, respect, uplifting and makes way for us to receive quick answers to our prayers.

Joseph's brothers hated him for their father's love for him. They could not say kind words to him. They planned to kill him even when he had their best interests at heart and was ready to sacrifice his time and effort for them. They were ready to part company with him and see him no more, because of their hatred for him. More so, they made up stories to cover up the wrongs they did to him. But it did not end there. What they did to Joseph made him go through other unpleasant situations. He was sold into slavery and he was also thrown into prison because Potiphar's wife told lies about him. He must have lived through years filled with a mixture of longing for his past home, times of hardship, frustration and regrets of his decision to have gone to check on his brothers as instructed by his father. This can be heart breaking. Yet, Joseph forgave his brothers.

We read from this chapter that Joseph recognised his brothers did not have a true knowledge of what their actions could have resulted in. They did not really know the implications of what they were doing. If they had known it, they would not have done it. If they knew their actions would have resulted in him ending up in the palace and being a ruler, they would not have sold him in the first place as they envied him.

People can plan wrong things against us but if we have a forgiving attitude, God always uses these as opportunities of blessings for us.

Also, Joseph recognised that upon all they did, they remembered him as a brother to them. This teaches us that although people may wrong us, they still remember the good we did to them prior to whatever might have happened. Some by reason of pride will not acknowledge it but know for sure all we have done for them. This can add to the extent of guilt they may have, realising they have paid back the good done to them with evil.

He also recognised they now knew what they did was wrong and should not have done it, probably because of the price they had to pay for their actions. But in all this, he decided to forgive them anyway.

People who offend us live with the guilt of what they have done and unless we forgive them, they cannot forgive themselves. Some might realise what they did and want to seek forgiveness but knowing the extent of what they have done and not knowing whether they will be accepted or not, they might find it difficult approaching and asking for forgiveness. Others will find it difficult asking for forgiveness because of pride and what people might say, just to mention a few. All these things further strain relationships and make it difficult for people who have offended us to want to relate to us again. In forgiving his brothers, Joseph was able to restore a broken relationship.

We learn forgiving others starts with a decision of wanting to let go of all that has been done to us no matter what the cost. Also, one will need to try to approach whoever has offended them and make themselves approachable. Joseph did things that made his brothers feel at ease and able to approach him. He gave them an opportunity to dine with him. Of course, it will be difficult for one to dine with someone you want to pay back with a good motive. But Joseph dined with them and held friendly conversations with them. He also expressed words of comfort rather than words of condemnation in a way as to help them forgive themselves. Through his actions he showed he had put behind him all that had happened and had forgiven them.

When we forgive others, we relieve ourselves of bitterness and pain that can have an effect on our health. Also, knowing unforgiveness is a seed of the devil, when we forgive others, it hinders the devil from having access to our lives. It also shows how mature we are in the things of God, and it makes people we forgive respect us more.

CHAPTER QUESTIONS

&

THEMES FOR THOUGHT

- What lessons can we learn from Joseph in relation to him forgiving his brothers?
- Why is it important to forgive people who offend us?
- What makes forgiving others difficult?
- What necessary steps can one take to forgive others?

YOU CAN SUMMARISE YOUR THOUGHTS

YOU CAN REVISIT YOUR THOUGHTS

CHAPTER 46

RELOCATION

So, Jacob left Beersheba, and his sons took him to Egypt. They carried him and their little ones and their wives in the wagons Pharaoh had provided for them. (NLT)

Genesis 46: 5

MESSAGE AND LEARNING

The thought of having to leave a place one has lived all their lives to start life all over again at a new place, makes people want to stay where they are without relocating, even when there is a need to do so. Most people get so attached to where they are and their current location, probably because of the comfort they enjoy, the hassle of moving belongings over, the relationships they have built over the years and also, the security they find in the jobs they have there. Others would rather not relocate for the fear of the unknown, that is whether or not they will be accepted where they are going or find the right job or be able to fulfil the purpose for which they are moving to this new place.

On the other hand, we find out that some people relocate so that they can be close to loved ones. Others are forced to move from where they are to other places due to adverse conditions such as wars, famine and pestilence. There are also others who relocate in the quest to find out what is on the other side, to experience new things, to have a mental break from where they are (that is if they are finding life in these areas challenging) and for want of a better life.

We read from chapter 26 of the book of Genesis of God's instruction to Isaac who had moved to the land of Gerar due to famine. God advised Isaac not to move from Gerar. Although, situations were not conducive in Gerar for Isaac and he feared losing his wife Rebecca in the land, he obeyed God. God had told him he was going to be with him and bless him there and God did just as he had promised. In the same chapter, we are told that Isaac sowed the land and that year his crops were tremendous. He reaped a hundred times more grain than he planted, for God blessed him until he became a rich man on the land. More importantly his wealth only continued to grow.

Here in this chapter, we read about God telling Jacob (Isaac's son), years down the line, not to be afraid to move out of the land of Canaan to Egypt. Just as God had promised Isaac, he was going to be with Jacob and bless him. Through his obedience to God and moving to Egypt, he and his family got to live on the best land in Egypt (Goshen). The land was fertile and was well watered by the river Nile. There they had enough pasture to feed their flock. Besides, they and their dependents, were furnished with adequate food by Joseph throughout the famine. Also, they were able to continue in their occupations as shepherds hence they maintained their original jobs. More importantly, Jacob was reunited with his son Joseph after such a long time of separation.

Having been presented with two choices in similar situations, I personally believe whatever choice one makes, that is whether to relocate or continue to stay at a particular place regardless of the circumstances that befall them, is entirely up to them. However, it will be wise to seek God's guidance in this matter as he knows all things: things that have occurred in the future, those now and ones yet to come. As although we can put careful thoughts into the need to relocate, where we would like to relocate to, the timings and circumstances, situations can overturn at any point in time and thereby influence whatever choices we are bound to make. By seeking God's guidance however, we get to make the best choice as to whether to relocate or not and are blessed with the choices we make as they are in accordance with his will, and avoid regrets.

What do you intend to do should you find circumstances where you live unfavourable? Relocate or not?

CHAPTER QUESTIONS

&

THEMES FOR THOUGHT

- What factors could influence your relocation?
- What factors could tie you down even when there is the need to relocate to another place in life?
- Why is seeking the will of God so prominent in relocating?

YOU CAN SUMMARISE YOUR THOUGHTS

YOU CAN REVISIT YOUR THOUGHTS

CHAPTER 47

SAVIOUR

"You have saved our lives!" they exclaimed. "May it please you, my lord, to let us be Pharaoh's servants."
(NLT)
Genesis 47: 25

MESSAGE AND LEARNING

A saviour is someone who helps, keeps safe or rescues another from harm, ruin or difficulty. Saviours are unique in the sense that they are selfless people who seek primarily to help others. They could be going through challenging situations themselves and yet have a deep concern for others rather than themselves. Although saviours are honoured in a lot of ways, being a saviour to others also comes at a cost in that one will need to sacrifice or pay a price in a way to achieve this aim. It could be sacrificing money, time or even energy to save the other person. In some cases, a saviour could help another person by offering emotional support to them as they go through tough times. Sometimes, it could be giving guidance or making the other person aware of an opportunity they could benefit from. At other times it could be lending a listening ear to the person and not necessarily saying or doing anything to help with the actual situation. There might also be the need to share resources other than money with others.

We learn from this chapter that Joseph was a saviour to his family and the whole nation of Egypt at a time when there was a food shortage in the lands of Canaan and Egypt. Previously he had interpreted the dreams of Pharaoh's cupbearer and chief baker and the cupbearer trusted that he will be able to interpret the Pharaoh's dreams in honesty as well. Hence, Joseph was sent for, was able to interpret the Pharaoh's dream and was put in charge of the affairs of food for the wisdom he displayed as God had revealed the interpretations of the Pharaoh's dreams through him. Joseph had foresight and a saving mentality in that, during Egypt's time of plenty, he ensured plans were made to reserve some food for later when there was famine: enough to feed all the Egyptians, people from other nations, his family who joined him in Egypt and their livestock. He sought the interest of the Pharaoh by buying all the people and their land for him without having a share in all he bought. Also, after providing the Egyptians with seeds to plant the fields, he allowed them to keep four-fifths of the harvest for themselves and the remainder was given to Pharaoh without him having any interest in the harvest received. Additionally, considering that

Joseph's brothers had wronged him by selling him into slavery, he forgave them and went ahead to save them. He did this by first, giving them food when they most needed it and putting their money back in their sacks without charging them for it. Secondly, he interceded for them with the Pharaoh so they and their livestock could settle on the land of Egypt. Thirdly, he purchased Goshen for them which was the best land on the Nile. All the things he did was to save them from the situations that befell them.

We can gather from this passage that saviours have certain unique characteristics besides their willingness to help others. They are selfless people in that, they give more attention and care to the needs of others compared to their own. Also, they are always ready to pay the price no matter what it takes to save a person. In addition, although they live in the present, they see beyond the present and plan for, and take wise considerations towards the future. This makes it possible for them to overcome present challenges with an aim of achieving their goals in life and place them in good stead to help others. By doing so, they find themselves in a better position to help others when the need arises. Furthermore, they are honest and trustworthy by nature, hence are easily approached by others for help and entrusted with crucial roles and responsibilities if need be. As well as that, saviours are wise people. and responsibilities if need be.

Another characteristic revealed in this passage specific to saviours is that they are forgiving people. It so often happens that the very people saviours are destined to save are the very ones who make it difficult for them to achieve this purpose. This maybe viewed as God's way of preparing them for the task ahead, and although God does not force people to do harm to others, he does allow such unpleasant circumstances to happen for his own purposes. It can be very challenging for the saviour however at their time of preparation. More so, it can be difficult for saviours to do what they need to do, when the time comes for them to save others, considering that a saviour might have faced certain unpleasant circumstances or hard times with the person or people, they are going to save having a hand in it. However, saviours can put the past behind them and go ahead to do what it takes to save the other person.

When a person is able to save others from their unpleasant situations, it can give them a sense of fulfilment in life and ensure both parties succeed. However, this should be done in the right way to ensure one does not burnout or put the person they are trying to save in a worse state than they already are.

Hence, why it is important that saviours have what it takes to save others before even attempting to do so.

Do you seem to identify with all or most of the characteristics mentioned above? Is there anyone around you whose salvation depends on you? Will you be willing to save your family, friends and others from difficulty, harm or ruin even if it will come at a price?

You could save the environment by doing your little bit not to pollute it. Also, you could save an unstable relationship by playing your part especially by forgiving those who hurt you. Similarly, you could save someone by giving them a hand or encouraging them when they need it.

Do you see yourself in a position of being able to help others or not?

CHAPTER QUESTIONS

&

THEMES FOR THOUGHT

- Knowing the cost of being a saviour, would you like to become one?
- What are some of the unique characteristics that may be seen in a saviour?
- Can you think of a time someone saved you out of a situation? What were your thoughts and feelings concerning the act of being saved?
- Being able to save other people produces a deep sense of fulfilment. Discuss.

YOU CAN SUMMARISE YOUR THOUGHTS

YOU CAN REVISIT YOUR THOUGHTS

CHAPTER 48

A BLISSFUL FAREWELL

Then Jacob said to Joseph, "Look, I am about to die, but God will be with you and will take you back to Canaan, the land of your ancestors. And beyond what I have given your brothers, I am giving you an extra portion of the land that I took from the Amorites with my sword and bow." (NLT)

Genesis 48: 21&22

MESSAGE AND LEARNING

It comes to a point in time when one has to say goodbye to colleagues, family or loved ones either forever or for a long time. But whether the separation is temporary or permanent, the impact of separation can be daunting. Depending on whom we say goodbye to and the circumstances surrounding the separation, it could be difficult, sorrowful or joyful. This chapter however deals with a farewell which although is normally considered to be sorrowful was bid in a blissful way.

Jacob realising his death was imminent, called for his son Joseph to bid him farewell. Although we are told his strength was failing rapidly, Jacob was able to gather his strength and sit up to greet him. It was at this time he had the chance to tell Joseph about particular things that happened to him while he journeyed through his life: how God had blessed him, the possessions he had acquired, who he will include in his inheritance and what he had planned to do before his death.

He shared his encounter with God and the promises God made to him with Joseph. God had promised to give Jacob and his descendants the land of Canaan as an everlasting possession, and Jacob was passing it on to them. Jacob gave Joseph an extra portion beyond what he had given his brothers and had plans of allowing Joseph's two sons Ephraim and Manasseh to inherit from him as well. Jacob also made Joseph aware of how he had given Rachel a befitting burial when situations were not conducive. Probably, portraying to him how a befitting burial could be given to a loved one and his expectations of how he should be buried.

We learn from this chapter that people more often than not bid farewell to those close to them, the people they relate to more at certain points in time. Probably because it gives them joy spending the time they have left with the people they feel loved by most. We also find out that people entrust their most treasured possessions to those they feel will take good care of them and not misuse what they have laboured for in their lifetime. As well as that, they share vital information with those they can trust and know will respect their wishes.

Jesus could have bid farewell to the entire world, but he chose to say goodbye to the world through his disciples (the few who were close to him) by making known his expectations to them and giving them a charge to keep. It was at this time he gave them the gift he had promised them, his spirit. He expected them to show forth his love through the way they acted towards each other and extend it to others. He wanted them to be united in all they did, so that together, they could make more disciples of him. In the same way, when Jacob was about to die, he sent for Joseph and his grandchildren to bid them farewell. This teaches us that although Jacob loved all his sons, he had a special affection for Joseph. Also, that, Joseph must have conducted himself in a way as to have won his father's affection.

In order to bid farewell in a blissful manner however, it is vital that one ensures there is peace between both parties that is the one bidding farewell and those being bid farewell. This is important because it ensures one can always revisit the friendly relationship once enjoyed, if both parties be alive and ever happen to reunite. In cases where one is lost through death, ensuring peace prior to the time the actual separation takes place is essential. This allows the survivor to live with a guilt free conscience, should there have been a misunderstanding in the relationship. Most importantly, it is vital we try and do what we possibly can, always for each other as each time we share could possibly be the last time we get to show kindness to the other party.

Would you rather bid farewell in a blissful manner or not?

CHAPTER QUESTIONS

&

THEMES FOR THOUGHT

- Bidding people farewell is a natural occurrence in life. True/ False?
- What makes it an uneasy thing to bid farewell to loved ones?
- What can we do to be able to bid a happy farewell to people?

YOU CAN SUMMARISE YOUR THOUGHTS

YOU CAN REVISIT YOUR THOUGHTS

CHAPTER 49

PARENT'S BLESSINGS

All these are the twelve tribes of Israel, and this is what their father said to them when he blessed them, giving each the blessing appropriate to him. (NIV)
Genesis 49: 28

MESSAGE AND LEARNING

Every blessing we enjoy comes from God. Some can be received directly from him, such as the gift of life, strength and the air we breathe. Others are channelled through a set means. One of which is through our parents, and this is one of the ways by which we can easily receive God's blessings however, the majority of us miss out on it. Probably as a result of sheer ignorance or because we are just not bothered to receive blessings through this way.

Parents are a blessing in themselves, in that they are the first contact through which God blesses us. God has chosen to use them as vessels through which we are birthed. We receive our existence from God through them and that is a blessing in itself. Besides this, we receive God's guidance and correction through our parents which opens doors for other blessings to come our way. More so, parents have the power to bless their children and whatever they say comes to pass. This explains why Esau having come back from preparing his father's favourite meal and realising Jacob had received his father's blessings could not help but cry for his father to bless him also. He knew of the power of a parent's blessings and what he can achieve from that. Hence, although Jacob took his father's blessings and left all the possessions he had behind, he knew he had taken the best and pleaded for what was left of the blessings to be given to him.

In this chapter we are presented with Jacob who gathers his children and pronounces blessings upon them. We learn that they were each blessed based on their actions to situations and their characters. Who they were, made them act the way they did. Their character birthed their conduct and this was shown in the way they reacted towards situations. This made them receive what they did. Another learning in relation to the topic at hand is that whatever blessings they received came to pass and was lasting.

To receive a parent's blessing however, it is important to do things to increase a parents' affection for one. Mainly, by doing things that will provoke blessings from our parents, we receive from them. Looking closely at the chapter we realise Reuben would have received a better blessing than he received, had it not been for his character. Reuben was the first born and should have received a greater of his father's blessings, the birth rite but for dishonouring his father's bed he did not receive them. Jacob described him as an unruly child. He was not one who submitted to the control and discipline of his father. He had a wayward character and behaved in a turbulent way which made him dishonour his father and lose a blessing he easily could have received. Simeon and Levi were the second and third in line to receive the blessing of a birth rite but because of their actions, they lost theirs as well. They acted in anger and violence, destroying innocent lives and bringing shame on their father. For this reason, Judah who was the fourth born received the blessing of a birth rite. As per the blessings received by the first born his brothers were to praise him, he was to defeat his enemies since he had received a blessing of power and authority and his relatives were to bow before him. Furthermore, kings and rulers were to come from his descendants from generation to generation. We get to know in further chapters that as a result of this blessing great rulers and kings including King David, Solomon and Jesus Christ were descendants of Judah.

When we dishonour our parent's, disobey and disrespect them and do things that bring them shame or hurt their feelings, we miss out on lots of blessings we could receive from them. However, there are many ways through which we can provoke a parent's blessing. Some of these are the opposite of what has already been mentioned. As well as that, we can take care of them and do things to protect their image or the family name so we can receive their blessings. Also, when we live to fulfil our God given destiny or are fulfilling it, thereby flourishing in all ways, it gives them joy. This can also provoke blessings from them.

Will you make the choice to do things to provoke the blessings of your parents or not?

CHAPTER QUESTIONS

&

THEMES FOR THOUGHT

- What is a parental blessing?
- What should you do in order to receive blessings from your parents?
- What kinds of attitudes could deprive a person of their parent's blessings?

YOU CAN SUMMARISE YOUR THOUGHTS

YOU CAN REVISIT YOUR THOUGHTS

CHAPTER 50

FULFILLING A PROMISE

So, his sons did for him just as he had commanded them. For his sons carried him to the land of Canaan and buried him in the cave of the field of Machpelah, before Mamre, which Abraham bought with the field from Ephron the Hittite as property for a burial place. (NKJV)

Genesis 50: 12&13

MESSAGE AND LEARNING

Certain situations demand that we make promises to others for the things we can do for them. At times, people also make promises to us of the things they will do for us. This gives us the assurance that what we expect to be done, will be done. Hence there is the need to honour the promises we make. God fulfils every promise he makes to us and expects us to do the same when we make promises. However, it is not always easy fulfilling a promise as it comes with paying a price of some sort. Sometimes, fulfilling a promise could cost you time, energy, money or other similar resources. Solomon therefore advises us in the book of Ecclesiastes in the Christian bible, not to make promises that we cannot fulfil.

Once we make a promise, we are bound to keep it and are expected to honour our word. This should make us slow to make promises but quick to honour them once they are made. In honouring a promise, we do what has been agreed upon at the time of making the promise. There might be specific details of what we have promised to do, and all these will have to be honoured. Besides this, the time of honouring the promise is equally important. If we fail to honour our promise at the expected time, it may distort already made plans, cause frustration and result in disappointments.

When we are able to fulfil a promise, people do not take our words lightly but rather they take whatever we say seriously. Also, we gain respect and trust from others by honouring our promises. Further to this, relationships can better be established when promises are honoured and others might be inspired to do the same, either by honouring a promise they have made to us or to someone else.

In the previous chapter we read about Joseph making a promise to his father regarding burying him in the cave in Ephron's field where Isaac and Abraham were buried.

Here in this chapter, we find out, he honours this promise. In doing so however, he needed the help of others, such as the morticians, who played the role of embalming his father's body to last the time until he was buried. Also, he had to seek the Pharaoh's permission for the time he was away to bury his father. Besides this, he had to part company with some of his family, the little ones for the time he was away. They journeyed days from Egypt to Canaan amidst mourning and holding a seven-day funeral for Jacob at Atad near the river Jordan and did as Jacob had commanded. Joseph did this to fulfil the promise he made to his father.

Later in the chapter, we find Joseph asks his brothers to make a promise to him to take his body with them and bury him in Canaan when God leads them out of Egypt into Canaan. As already mentioned, by honouring the promise he made to his father, Joseph's brothers would have been inspired to do the same for him. That is, honour the promise they made to him to take his body with them to Canaan. He would have earned his brothers respect, loyalty and trust as they would have developed a positive perception of him through his act of honouring the promise he made to his father.

In all, Joseph fulfilled the promise he made to his father by doing all Jacob commanded and at the time he was expected to do it while forfeiting other commitments he had. This might have cost him in several ways, yet he did all he promised to, and this gave him the courage to ask his brothers to do the same for him.

Would you endeavour to honour the promises you make moving forwards?

CHAPTER QUESTIONS

&

THEMES FOR THOUGHT

- How will you feel when a promise that was made to you was not fulfilled?
- Fulfilling a promise could cost us in certain ways. Can you identify some of these ways? Why is it always important to fulfil the promises we make to people?

YOU CAN SUMMARISE YOUR THOUGHTS

YOU CAN REVISIT YOUR THOUGHTS

REFERENCES

Abuelaish, I. & Arya, N. (2017). Hatred-a public health issue. *Medicine, conflict and survival*, *33*(2), 125-130.